We Don't Look Like What We've Been Through

Testimonies of Kingdom Women: Powerful, Purposeful and Precious

An Anthology

Volume 1

By: Tiffany L. Henderson
and
The Kingdom Advancement Center Women

© Copyright 2018 – The Kingdom Advancement Center, Inc.

All rights reserved. This book is protected by the copyright laws of the United States of America. No part of this publication may be reproduced, stored in a retrieval system, or transmitted in any form or by any means – electronic, mechanical, digital, photocopy, recording, or any other – except for brief quotations in printed reviews, without the prior permission of the publisher. Unless otherwise identified, Scripture quotations are from the King James Version of the Bible.

All emphasis within the Scripture quotations is the author's own.

Cover by Mpressive Graphics

WE DON'T LOOK LIKE WHAT WE'VE BEEN THROUGH

TESTIMONIES OF KINGDOM WOMEN: POWERFUL, PURPOSEFUL AND PRECIOUS, AN ANTHOLOGY

Copyright © 2018

The Kingdom Advancement Center, Inc.

378 Division Street

Elgin, Illinois 60120

www.thekingdomac.com

Published by: KAC Publishing

ISBN-13: 978-0692195314

ISBN-10: 0692195319

Acknowledgements

The Women of the Kingdom Advancement Center would like to thank:

Our Abba Father, El Elyon, the Most High God, for His unconditional love, wisdom, guidance and life! To our Savior, Jesus the Christ, who died and rose that we might be free to live the life the Father gave us, Thank you! Your love towards us knows no bounds and we commit our lives to serving you for the rest of our lives!

To our Apostle and Senior Pastor, Larry Henderson, Jr. – thank you for being a valiant, fearless, visionary that leads us with Apostolic fervor and might. You tenaciously, patiently and strategically impart into all of us with the love of a father and for that, we thank you! We love you Apostle!

To our Kingdom Advancement Center Family – we love you!! Thank you for encouraging us to write the vision and make it plain upon tablets that they may run that read it! We have an amazing church family made of people who genuinely love and care for one another. You are a rare gem that we will not take for granted.

To all of our husbands, children, family, friends, co - workers and loved ones – thank you for your love, support, friendship, and prayers. It means the world to us! We all need each other and you all have helped us through some of the most difficult seasons of our lives and for that, we thank you!

Special thank you to Tamika Law and AtteniL Management Group for their priceless edits!!

Table of Contents

Foreword 9
Introduction 11

PART I: THE POWER OF PRAYER **15**

Presumed Dead, But Alive and Well
By: Teresa Price 17

My Story, His Faithfulness
By: Kim Gillam 20

Breach of Faith
By: Korei Mullins 27

Overcoming Sexual Assault and Self-Harm
By: Amber Meyer 31

Our Identity
By: Taylor Bradford 35

None Shall Be Barren
By: Gloria Golden 39

Hope: Your Expectation For Tomorrow!
By: Minister Crystal L. Bradford 46

By His Stripes I am Healed
By: Synesha Parish 52

The Power of Prayer: Questions for Reflection/Discussion **56**

PART II: LIVING LIFE ON PURPOSE **59**

Listening To God and Finding Your Voice
By: Minister Quiana Kee 61

Redefining Success
By: Suzanne Brockner 66

Preparation Opens the Door for God's Manifestation
By: Brianna Bradford 73

Raising the Bar
By: Prophet Tiffany L. Henderson 79

College Changes Everything
By: Kimberly Shaw 84

Workplace Miracles
By: Shelia Roberts 92

Choose Christ
By: Denise Hartung – Manuel 97

In The Fight For My Life
By: Roselyn Forbes 100

Living Life on Purpose: Questions for Reflection/Discussion **108**

PART III: WE ARE PRECIOUS IN HIS SIGHT **111**

STILL STANDING!
By: ANONYMOUS 113

From My Back to My Knees!
By: Kellie Murphy 117

Have You Considered…
By: Minister Nikki Palmer 123

Believe Only! When Your Back is Against the Wall
By: Brenda J. Law 132

My Steps are Ordered by the Lord
By: Tiffin Horton 137

Finding LIFE in CHRIST through DEATH...of both my Parents
By: Kriste N. Clayton 140

YOU ARE NO ACCIDENT
By: Sonia Ivy..146

Leaving It All to Follow Jesus
By: Mandy Garcia..149

We Are Precious In His Sight: Questions for Reflection/Discussion 153

Epilogue 155

Foreword
Apostle Larry Henderson, Jr.

And I heard a loud voice saying in heaven, Now is come salvation, and strength, and the kingdom of our God, and the power of his Christ: for the accuser of our brethren is cast down, which accused them before our God day and night. **And they overcame him by the blood of the Lamb, and by the word of their testimony;** *and they loved not their lives unto the death. (Romans 12:10-11)*

And we know that all things work together for good to them that love God, to them who are the called according to his purpose. (Romans 8:28)

God is always trying to lead us to His Word. His utmost desire is that we live our lives according to His will. His will is in His Word. He wants to see us live faithful lives according to His Word. He wants to say, "Well done my good and faithful servant!" He knows His will is best for our lives.

However, oft times, like children, we are not convinced His way is best. We believe that all of the Father's rules, laws, and precepts are restricting our freedom. They are quenching our fun. He is not giving us the things we want as quickly as we want to receive them. His ways seem slow. Sin seems more fun, more quickly. We want gratification instead of strategy and the path of least resistance instead of discipline. It is too hard to serve Jesus, first. Our way seems best. We want to have one foot in the world and the other being blessed by God. We begin to feel these are mutually exclusive. We cannot see that God's way will bring us more joy.

Because we cannot see the forest for the trees, that God's will for us will cause us to be more fulfilled, quite often each of us must experience God-ordered trials and tribulations on the way to our miracle. We all have our own path to salvation. God often, if not always, uses our circumstances to lead us back to His will for our lives and into His presence. God wants us to discover his Word for our lives. He wants us to discover it of our own will. He wants His Word to become our Testimony.

In this book Tiffany Henderson has done an excellent job to capture the testimony of the saints! The Kingdom belongs to the saints (Daniel 7:18). More importantly, she has captured the Word of the testimony of these amazing women of God. Quite often we have learned to testify, but we have not learned to testify with the Word that brings us healing and deliverance. This is called the Word of our Testimony. In other words, what is the Word of God the Lord has been trying desperately to share with us that is the source of God's thoughts, peace, and future for us (Jeremiah 29:11)? This is the reason for our trials, the fulfillment of the will of God in our lives to bring us back to His life giving Word.

... And they overcame Him ... by the Word of their testimony!

Larry Henderson, Jr.
Senior Overseer, The Kingdom Advancement Center
Elgin, IL
Author of The Revelation of Healing

Introduction

"First giving honor to God who is the head of my life…" This was usually the opening sentence to every testimony service in churches across America. Folks would stand up and lift their hands to testify about the goodness of the Lord and all He had done in their lives. It was the Power of the Testimony that gave strength to weary souls and reinforced the belief that God was able and willing to work miracles on their behalf. Most testimonies would end by saying, "If He did it for me, I know, He can do it for you! Y'all pray my strength in the Lord." It was this ray of hope offered by the testifier that let the hearer know, God did something great for someone else and He could certainly do it for them as well. He is no respecter of persons.

Over time, the art of testifying became lost. Churches stopped having testimony service and essentially blocked one of the greatest tools for deliverance. The bible says in Revelation 12:11, *And they overcame him by the blood of the Lamb, and by the word of their testimony; and they loved not their lives unto the death.* It was by the blood of the Lamb AND the word of their testimony that caused God's people to overcome the accuser of the brethren, the one who accused them before God day and night (Revelation 12:10). Our testimony is a tool God gives us to encourage one another that He is faithful to perform every word He has spoken, to fulfill every promise made and do exceeding, abundantly above all that we could ever ask or imagine, according to the power that works in us! The bible refers to the Power of the Testimony over and over again. In Exodus, when God gave Moses the commandment and the dimensions for the Ark of the Covenant, he was sure to include the Testimony:

And thou shalt put into the ark the testimony which I shall give thee. (Exodus 25:16)

And thou shalt put the mercy seat above upon the ark; and in the ark thou shalt put the testimony that I shall give thee. (Exodus 25:21)

And there I will meet with thee, and I will commune with thee from above the mercy seat, from between the two cherubims which are upon the ark of the testimony, of all things which I will give thee in commandment unto the children of Israel. (Exodus 25: 22)

The testimony was so important to God that He made sure to include it in His covenant with the children of Israel. The Ark of the Testimony was meant to be a reminder of the goodness of the Lord, His faithfulness toward His children and His promises for them. This testimony went with the children of Israel everywhere they went, even into battle. As long as they had the Testimony, they had no reason to fear their enemies, for they knew the Lord was with them.

It is with this in mind that this book was written. The women of The Kingdom Advancement Center understand the power of the testimony and want to testify of the goodness of the Lord to edify, exhort and comfort others who may be similarly situated. This idea was birthed at our women's retreat in May 2018. While in our session on prayer, testimony after testimony was released speaking on how prayer changed their lives. Many were healed, delivered and set free within that very hour. While speaking to a woman there and hearing her testimony I heard the

Introduction

Lord say "Anthology," repeatedly. I didn't quite know what He wanted me to do with the information, but He was relentless in His pursuit to get me to acknowledge His words. Finally, after the "testimony session," I realized what the Lord wanted us to do. He wanted us to write our collective testimonies as one large Testament to His power and might.

Indeed, the Lord has been good to the women of The Kingdom Advancement Center. We are women of varying shades of beauty, wrapped in unique filters of race, age, educational degrees, socio-economic status, family identities and life experiences. The eternal tie that binds us all is despite what we have been through, we all radiate the splendor of His grace, mercy and love that covers a multitude of sins! This grace makeover is creating a flawless finish better than MAC or Cover Girl could ever conceive and we are shining brighter every day! To be sure, we don't look like what we've been through!

Finally, there is a testimony for everyone who reads this book. Whether you jump around or read straight through, there is a Word from God waiting for you. It is our sincere prayer, as you read this Anthology, that you too might increase in hope, strength and faith that the Lord our God is indeed with you. If He did it for us, He can do it for you too!

-Prophet Tiffany L. Henderson

We Don't Look Like What We've Been Through

PART I
THE POWER OF PRAYER

And he spake a parable unto them to this end, that men ought always to pray, and not to faint; (Luke 18:1)

Confess your faults one to another, and pray one for another, that you may be healed. The effectual fervent prayer of a righteous man availeth much. Elias was a man subject to like passions as we are, and he prayed earnestly that it might not rain: and it rained not on the earth by the space of three years and six months. And he prayed again, and the heaven gave rain, and the earth brought forth her fruit. (James 5: 16-18)

Jesus was very clear in Luke that men should always pray and not faint. He wanted the disciples to understand the importance and urgency of prayer in their lives. He went on to fortify this point by using the example of the unjust judge that granted a widow what she needed because she continued to bombard him with her requests (Luke 18: 1-8). The idea is that we must Pray Until Something Happens. PUSH!! Don't stop praying until you see the *effects* of prayer. The effect of the widows prayer was the judge avenged her of her adversary.

This is also the principle by which Elijah prayed. The bible says he was a man like us and prayed earnestly that it might not rain, and it did not rain. The most important lesson to learn from Elijah was that his "earnest prayer" was just a pronouncement that it would not rain based on the Word he received from God. That is all! (Read I Kings 17 and 18. It is quite hilarious yet very impactful). He made a decree that it would not rain except by his word, and it did not rain! The bible calls that an earnest prayer!! It's the kind of prayer packed with so much power (faith) that it commands the weather! That is the power of prayer! Elijah stood flat – footed on the Word of God and did not waiver. He was so confident in the Word he heard from God that he was willing to face ridicule, shame and death to see it come to pass. This is what it means to be fervent and effectual through the prayer of faith.

In Part I, you will read stories of miracles, faith and healing through the power of prayer. The women in this section survived a horrific car accident, was miraculously healed of a tumor, overcome disorders, healed and delivered from addiction and abuse, increased faith through prophetic revelation and much more. Their testimonies are powerful because we can see through prayer, angelic help, prophetic impartation and deliverance how their lives were changed, their faith increased and God was glorified!

Presumed Dead, But Alive and Well
By: Teresa Price

The angel of the LORD encampeth round about them that fear him, and delivereth them. (Psalm 34:7)

On Friday, June 21, 2009, at 1:15 p.m. in the afternoon; it was a beautiful sunny day, with not one cloud in the sky. I was driving along the vacant highway in my four-passenger dark blue 190E Mercedes-Benz automobile. I was playing my Christian music as I was driving, learning the lyrics in order to prepare to "lip sing" for the Women's Day program that was quickly approaching. Apparently, I should only sing in the shower because I do not have an angelic voice, so I've been told! At any rate, my automobile was enveloped with spiritual Joy. Suddenly, an eighteen-wheeled truck appeared in my rear view mirror snaking across the highway behind my car. I began screaming: "Where are the traffic police? He is intoxicated!! He is drunk!! Why is this man driving in this condition? He has been drinking!! He is going to hit my automobile!!" Sitting on the shoulder of the highway to the right of my vehicle, was another eighteen-wheeled truck; then I fainted and blacked out.

As I began to regain consciousness, I could hear loud clanging, glass breaking, and what sounded like explosions, as if weapons were being fired. It made me feel as if I was on a battlefield in the middle of a war. The "war" that seemingly surrounded me was my vehicle being rammed into the illegally parked eighteen-wheeled truck on the shoulder of the Highway. My vehicle was rammed until the top of my automobile was sliced like a loaf of bread and peeled off like tin on a can. Miraculously, the Lord my God placed my driver seat in a supine position as if I was lying flat, facing upward in my bed. The top of my car was sliced off because of how I was rammed into the back of the truck and my head should have been decapitated, but by the grace of God my body remained fully intact. My mom appeared to me as an angel with her arms folded shaking her head like something had happened to me, as if I was once again that clumsy teenager when being scoured. "You'll be alright!!" I heard her say. I was delighted to see my Mom's spirit again. I was comforted by her love and words of encouragement as only she could give. It was at that moment that reality crept in and I was awakened by the voices of Firemen and Police Officers. "She's dead!...Wait! No, she's alive!" I heard the emergency workers going back and forth about whether or not I was alive. It was then I thought to speak. I simply stated, "If you call my husband and my two daughters, I will be fine, but I am experiencing horrific pain." The air bags broke all ten of my fingers and there was blood everywhere, my hands were very bloody as I lost my small left finger. The first responders had to extricate me from the vehicle through sawing and cutting and once freed, I was immediately rushed to the hospital and prepped for the first of thirteen hand surgeries.

Interestingly, after I awakened from surgery, I asked my doctor "where is my finger? I want my finger!" I was not focused on being alive. Clearly, God saved me and all I could think about at that time was my pinky finger! While in the hospital, my appearance was that of a Mummy, wrapped in white bandages from my neck to my waist to ensure my hands healed properly. I had many visitors from the public wanting to witness the person that survived "The accident." I was released from the hospital one week later. I was clearly a walking, talking, breathing physical miracle to be in a car accident with the top completely sliced off and the only thing that was affected was my hands. The bible says, *The angel of the LORD encamps round about them that fear him, and delivers them.* The Lord clearly delivered me, saved my life and I love Him all the more for it! To God be the Glory!

My Story, His Faithfulness
By: Kim Gillam

Now faith is the substance of things hoped for, the evidence of things not seen. For by it the elders obtained a good report. (Hebrews 11: 1, 2)

I lived with my Gram who was like a mom to me for as far back as I can remember. I lived with her most of my life until she passed away in January of 1990. This is where my story begins. In late 1989 early 1990, I began dating this guy. His friend invited me to a youth group. I was not saved at the time. It was through this youth group that I met and received the love of the Father and made a commitment to follow Him. I am not sure how it happened, but I am eternally grateful it did.

In January of 1990 my Gram was hospitalized and ended up passing away at the end of the month. Before she passed, she made a few comments about the possibility of me being pregnant. I suspected I might be, but I was not sure. My Gram knew, and she suggested I not go through with the pregnancy because she would not be able to help. As I considered this I went to the doctor and confirmed that I was indeed pregnant. I decided to go ahead and have the baby and trust the Lord. Suddenly, I found myself pregnant, alone and homeless. I was able to find a temporary place with my mother until I delivered the baby and moved out on my own. I was 20 years old, insecure in my faith, angry and scared.

By August of 1990 it was time for my child to be born. I was excited, anxious, and nervous all at the same time. I went to the hospital like any other expectant mother and went through labor and delivery. After many hours, I gave birth to a beautiful boy! As soon as he was born I knew something was not right. I was waiting for the doctor to give me the baby to hold since that's usually what they do, but that didn't happen. I began to worry as I waited for the nurses to bring me my son. The doctors and nurses were examining him and after what seemed like a lifetime they informed me that he was born with a diaphragmatic hernia (a defect or hole in the diaphragm that allows the abdominal contents to move into the chest cavity). Basically, things were not in the right place and needed to be corrected. So, at three hours old my beautiful newborn baby boy was hooked up to a machine and transferred to another hospital. I sat there so confused, trying to figure out what happened! I had a normal pregnancy with no issues the entire nine months. The doctors said that even if they knew ahead of time, nothing could have been done before he was born. I'm just glad they reacted so quickly once he was born.

The first couple of nights after my baby was born were rough because I was at one hospital and he was at another and I could not be there for him. I was still grieving the loss of my Gram and I began thinking that I could lose my son as well. All I remember is crying the whole time asking God why this happened (remember I was a new Christian)? I was missing my Gram and I felt alone and sad at a time when I should have been the happiest. I did not understand.

I pleaded and prayed that he would be ok and that I would not lose him too. My son needed a miracle and God was the only one who could provide it for him. All I wanted was to be with him. Finally, after several days I was released from the hospital and told to go home and continue to rest. I went straight to the other hospital to be with my son and that is where we spent the next 4 months.

The doctor's surgically corrected the hernia my son was born with and immediately placed him on an "echmo," which is a heart/lung bypass machine. He was also on oxygen and feeding tubes as he was sedated heavily at the beginning. He was eventually taken off the bypass machine, but still needed the oxygen to help him breath until he could breathe on his own. At some point, my baby contracted an infection through a central line, which in turn, caused him to be stricken with spinal meningitis, which led to seizures. The case was so severe the doctors asked me if the seizures continued, did I want them to resuscitate him. They also explained that if he were to survive he would be a "vegetable" or in a vegetative state. Of course I said yes! I thought to myself, "How could they ask me that? This is my child and I am going to love him and take care of him no matter what!"

As time went by, he slowly became better. When he was about 2 months old I was allowed to hold him for the very first time and try to feed him with a bottle. It was nice to hold him but scary at the same time, because he was still connected to many tubes. Feeding from a bottle was a struggle for him. Eventually he gained enough strength and weight that the doctors were ready to release him from the hospital. Before he was released the doctors emphasized my need to learn infant CPR due to him still being prone to seizures. I also needed to learn how to put in his feeding tube and work the machine along with the oxygen tanks because he would be going home with all these things. Even with all of that, it was the best news ever!!!

In December of 1990, my baby boy finally came home. It was such a blessing, even if I had to watch him closely to make sure he did not have a seizure. As part of his daily regiment, I had to check that his oxygen levels were good and that he did not pull out his feeding tube. He did have a few setbacks and as scary as they were at the time, we made it through. He eventually stopped having seizures and was taken off all seizure medications. He was also off the feeding tube and oxygen. All of the other complications (spinal meningitis, infections and seizures) are what caused him to have a developmental delay and hearing loss, but my child was not a "vegetable!" It was a miracle! The doctor's expected the worse, but we believed God for His best! We prayed for a miracle and received one!

During my son's early years in school, he needed lots of speech, physical and occupational therapy to help him along his journey. After kindergarten, we moved from the city to the suburbs so he could go to a school that had a deaf/hard of hearing program. In this program he would not only use speech, which he does well with the amount of hearing loss he has, he would also learn sign language which he would need to communicate better. Throughout school we tried him in regular classes, but it seemed he needed to be in self-contained classes which were smaller in size and along with academics, the program taught him "real life" skills. We had our issues as all parent/child relationships do, like him wanting to have more freedom and independence. Those struggles were hard because he was not able to understand my concern for his safety. Through time I was able to give him a little more freedom and we worked it out with a lot of tears and prayers. My son was able to graduate from high school and hold down a job.

At the age of 18, I petitioned for guardianship of him since he was not capable of managing his own finances, cook on his own or go to a doctor by himself. I was awarded full guardianship. In October of 2013 he was given the opportunity to move into a facility for people with disabilities. This is something I never thought would happen, but it did. This was another way of seeing God move. This facility was near me and he was still able to visit me on the weekends. The purpose of this place was to provide him with a sense of independence and freedom. The home was supervised 24 hours a day and my son would be able to continue learning the "life skills" he needed to eventually move to a different facility with intermittent staff. The transition to this place was rough for both of us and I continued to trust God that all things would work out.

Our lives changed again in January 2014. It was a cold, stormy, icy day when no one should have been out on the roads. At 2:14 am I was awakened by a call from my son who proceeded to tell me that he was in an accident. I was frantic and immediately began to worry! He told me not to worry because a friend was going to bring him home. After enough time had passed and I thought he should've been home, I tried to call and received no answer. I then called his "house" to see if he was there and the staff told me no. I completely freaked out! "Where is my son? Is he alright?" I thought to myself. I continued to try and reach him or the person he was with to no avail until finally I connected with a nurse! She told me the name of the hospital and I begged her not to let him leave with anyone because I would be there to pick him up. It would take me an hour to get there which felt like a lifetime. On the way, I did not know how severe his injuries were but I did know that he was the only one who was hurt in that accident. Everyone else escaped free of injury.

Once I arrived, I was told of his injuries…he broke his neck. I was shocked and totally devastated! How could this have happened? Will he be okay? I immediately called my family members and let them know what happened. I began asking them to pray and have their church pray for him. Then I began to pray! He had to be transferred to another hospital to have neck surgery and there we found ourselves having to spend time in the hospital, again. This time, however, was much shorter and the recovery not as long. Thankfully he was not paralyzed and I was told it could have been much worse. God was moving. The surgery went well, as did his recovery. The doctors were impressed at how well things went from surgery to recovery. He had to have therapy to learn to walk and balance himself again before he left the hospital, but he was able to walk out of the hospital!

He continued to gain his strength back once he left the hospital, but he became very angry and distant. I wanted to help him but didn't know how. We then visited the KAC to see an old friend. We enjoyed it so much we started attending regularly. While we really loved this church, my son was somewhat limited in what he could understand during service. While at a conference held at the church, a woman attended from Washington DC. She was a Professional Sign Language Interpreter and signed the entire conference to my son, sharing the Good News of the gospel to him in such a way that he could understand what was being said. As a result, he gave his life to the Lord!

Since that day, he has never been happier than what he is right now! His anger is gone, he sings, claps and dances before the Lord with all his might! I am just overjoyed! The Lord has truly been faithful to us both! Throughout all of life's tragedies, trials and tribulations, I can clearly see how God showered his love and faithfulness. As I have walked this journey, I have to admit that my faith wavered at times, but I always knew that my son would be fine. My God is an awesome and faithful God even in our times of doubt. He has increased my faith and shown me just how much he loves us.

Breach of Faith
By: Korei Mullins

Satan desires to have you, that he may sift you as wheat but I have prayed for you, that your faith fail not (Luke 22:31-32)

I have learned that one of the most difficult things for kingdom citizens to reconcile is the hurt and disappointment from seemingly unanswered prayers or more simply, prayers that are not answered in the way that we desire. It is hard to accept when the outcome is something other than what you believed God for and you are struggling to reconcile that breach of faith. It becomes a common practice to do an assessment of sorts, a multi-point inspection; "Did I have faith? Was I standing on the scriptures that best addressed my situation? Was there praying and fasting, an agreement with other believers or bold declarations made?" For me, I have had two up close and personal times where my faith was radical and I doggedly believed God for the healing and deliverance of two loved ones, yet the outcome was far from what I expected. Then doubt began to set in and other people will exasperate that doubt with explanations of why they believe healing or deliverance did not take place. One thing that I have learned is that no matter what, there is a blessing in continuing on and knowing that we do not serve a High Priest that does not sympathize with us (Hebrews 4:15) and that he is interceding at the right hand of the Father for us (Romans 8:34).

When Jesus tells Peter in Luke 22:31-32, that "Satan not only desires him but to also sift him as wheat," it cannot be lost on the reader that not only does Satan want us but he wants us broken all the way down; he wants our faith, belief in God and his promises to disintegrate into the lowest form so that there is no bringing it back together. The enemy wants our faith to fail and not just one time but multiple times. He wants us to give up so that he can talk us out of the promises of God, but we must continue to believe. For that one prayer that seemingly went unanswered, you must look at the other prayers that were answered.

I knew some years ago that I likely had some undiagnosed fertility issues because there were sufficient instances where if I could have become pregnant, I would have. I began to lower my expectations surrounding having children. I became more undecided and indifferent, then my mother became ill and subsequently passed away and I was convinced that I didn't want children without having my mother here with me.

I began talking myself out of motherhood, while simultaneously receiving prophetic word after prophetic word about my womb being opened and giving birth. I was confused. I had all but given up on the idea until I finally decided to have a battery of tests to see what I was up against concerning my fertility. My gynecologist told me due to my age and what she diagnosed as fibroids and Polycystic Ovarian Syndrome (PCOS), that I needed to see a fertility specialist immediately. I scoured over fertility specialists and there was only one that I was drawn to and he had a lengthy waiting list and once I was on the list, he went out sick for several months. My faith attempted to fail but the prophetic words continued to be spoken in my life.

My fertility doctor needed to create his own profile of my fertility and this took some time, because it requires monthly monitoring of various fertility markers. There were weekly tests and a lot of waiting. One particular month, I was taking a long time to ovulate, there were tests that needed to be run but they could not pinpoint my ovulation. I had to continue to come in to be checked for my time of ovulation. During one such appointment, much to the nurse's dismay, I only had one egg follicle present. This is significant because even for fertility treatment to be administered, there has to be a minimum of five follicles. The nurse was rather dismissive and told me to call her when I started to menstruate.

After a few weeks, I called to ask a question and mentioned that I had not yet had my cycle. The nurse went back to my charts and said, "Well, you did have one follicle. If you don't have your cycle within a week, take a pregnancy test and let us know the results." I waited a week, took the pregnancy test and it was positive! I called the fertility doctor and they scheduled me to come in and their follow up tests confirmed that I was indeed six weeks pregnant.

God is so awesome in that even though I created a mental stronghold about my ability to conceive, He was still faithful! I used the prophecies that had gone before me to fight a good warfare (1 Timothy 1:18). I stood on the Logos and Rhema Word of God to move me from faith to faith and as long as I was moving with my faith, the possibilities for a breach decreased. My testimony is such that while trying to generate my fertility profile/plan, I was able to conceive without any fertility treatment! Take heart today and know that Jesus has prayed for us, that our faith fail not!

Overcoming Sexual Assault and Self-Harm
By: Amber Meyer

If the Son therefore shall make you free, ye shall be free indeed. (John 8:36)

    When I was eight years old, my life took a tragic turn after I was molested by two cousins. The molestation was ongoing and something that my young mind could not fully comprehend. Both of my parents come from large families that regularly gathered for holidays, birthdays, and other special occasions. It would be during these family gatherings that I was violated time and time again. After five years of enduring the pain and confusion of these assaults, I decided to take a stand against my cousins. I was threatened and manipulated to believe that it was my fault because I had long blonde hair and blue eyes that was too desirable for them to resist. They further convinced me to keep quiet by telling me that no one would believe me and that I would tear the family apart. In that moment, I not only accepted defeat, I accepted the weight of guilt, shame, and embarrassment. Without the proper skills or outlet, I did the only thing I could think of to cope, I attempted to suppress my emotions.

    I began dating at 15 years old. My first boyfriend was also my best friend and I fell in love with him. As we became more serious, all of the trauma and bad memories that I tried to suppress began to resurface. This was the onset of my panic/anxiety attacks, flashbacks, and nightmares.

Overwhelmed with the onslaught of pain and anguish, my self-destruction commenced. I began drinking alcohol, smoking marijuana, cutting myself, and eventually attempted suicide. After my suicide attempt, I was checked into a mental facility where I learned that my addiction to cutting myself was a form of disassociation. The pain from cutting would temporarily distract me from the pain of the past.

Shortly after turning 16 years old, my neighbor and older brother's best friend raped me. What made this more devastating is that he was someone I trusted and even confided in about my childhood molestation. He was a family friend and I always thought it was cool to be around him. I would even occasionally babysit his son. I felt safe enough with him to sneak out the house to drink and smoke with him but the night he raped me, someone laced my drink with the date rape drug, GHB also known as Liquid G. This drug paralyzed me. I was in and out of consciousness with limited recollection of what all happened to me in the basement of his home. When I regained consciousness and mobility, I gathered my belongings and cried all the way home.

The guilt, shame, and embarrassment from my childhood was now back in full force, I was now spiraling. I called my boyfriend and he encouraged me to tell my parents. Thankfully my parents believed me and called the police which was followed by the hospital for a rape kit. The police did not doubt my story, however, the difficulty of proving the case became an issue when the DNA kit yielded inconclusive results. It was determined that the case was not strong enough to move forward and once again, I felt victimized and helpless.

From that experience, I developed Post-Traumatic Stress Disorder (PTSD) and this was in addition to the anxiety/panic attacks, cutting, and suicide attempts. I was hospitalized 38 times for self-harm and suicidal behavior. Throughout my teenage years, I battled anorexia and bulimia, which resulted in life long issues with weight. I did experience an early breakthrough with the eating disorders and recognized that as the power of God at work in my life. The pain from childhood and adolescence held on to me like a vice grip and followed me into adulthood where I continued down a destructive path in an effort to numb the pain and block out the memories. There were constant triggers that would send me reeling, from seeing men that resembled my molesters to smells or situations; I would relive the rape as if it was just happening. I was terrified of men and did not trust anyone. I was nearing rock bottom.

The bottom for me came when I was confronted with the consequences of my self-destructive behavior and that resulted in losing custody of my children. The only bright spot in my life, the light in my perpetual darkness, and the last bit of hope that I held on to was now taken from me. I was lower than low with no hope, peace, or joy, abandoned, an outcast, and rejected by those around me. I had nothing to live for and I planned to take my life but God intervened in a mighty way when I could not go through with my plan. There was a strong urging and conviction, I felt the presence of God like never before and I knew that this was not his will for me.

In 2012, I began going to church and accepted Jesus Christ as my Lord and Savior. This was not a smooth transition as I initially struggled to sit through an entire service but with time, I grew stronger in the Lord and in his Word. The scriptures became life to me and I spoke them out loud and believed them. I knew that God had given me beauty for my ashes and that He had come to bind up my wounds. God had not forsaken me! He died for me because He loved me! I began regularly attending bible study, praying, seeking God with my whole heart and I noticed that my faith increased and was abounding.

The power of God was moving in my life, healing and deliverance was taking place. As the word of God declares, *If the Son therefore shall make you free, ye shall be free indeed* (John 8:36). I was set free from sexual assault, anxiety/panic attacks, self-harm and PTSD. Suicidal thoughts were replaced with thoughts of abundant life. The Lord also used counseling and support groups to aid in my recovery. I was always blessed that the Lord would position another believer by my side to uplift, encourage, and bring me comfort during the difficult times of healing and deliverance. He even restored my relationship with my children.

I am an overcomer and I pray that by sharing my testimony that someone will believe that God is not a respecter of persons, what he did for me, he will certainly do for you. Just as he saved and transformed me from the inside out, the same supernatural power of God is available to you.

Our Identity
By: Taylor Bradford

So God created man in his own image, in the image of God created he him; male and female created he them. (Genesis 1:27)

There are multiple experiences in my life that have shaped my identity; from relationships to medical challenges and so on. One in particular that I want to focus on was my battle with Attention Deficit Disorder (A.D.D).

Around the third grade I was diagnosed with Attention Deficit Disorder and as a kid, that diagnosis had a very large impact on me. With even the softest use of words, hearing the diagnosis that I needed medicine, in order to reach the same level as everyone else rang in my ears. (This diagnosis as a child meant that I needed medication to be like everyone else.)

Throughout my childhood I had a heart for helping others. When I started middle school, I saw a flyer at a camp I attended. On the flyer they were seeking children with "normal brain function" to run tests that would allow them to learn more about children with autism. I thought this would be a great idea so I asked my mom to sign me up. I can still remember my heart sinking to my stomach when my mom got off the phone telling me I wouldn't be able to participate because of my A.D.D. I was devastated as every thought of rejection rushed through my mind. "Why couldn't I be enough to help these children?" (I thought I was normal.) Questioning if I would ever be able to measure up to a "normal person;" if I would ever fit in with "normal children." Throughout middle school and high school, quarterly Psychologist visits and pill dosage evaluations became a regular thing. 40 mg in the morning, 20 mg boost every afternoon before homework, before sports practice; and an increase on my medication before finals week. With this being my daily routine for 10 years, I began to feel that it defined me. If I ever forgot to take my medicine in the morning my mood would immediately drop. I truly felt like I was incapable of doing regular activities or socially interacting without it. I even switched medications a few times due to feeling overwhelmed and stressed.

In August of 2015, I went away to college and for the first time taking my medicine just didn't feel right to me. I began studying (thanks to my Kingdom Institute classes) about the dominion that God has given us to live above our circumstances and who I was created to be in Him. One Sunday in September I tuned into my church service back home through FaceTime and our Apostle prompted the church to stretch their faith and pick a few days out of the week to fast. It wasn't recommended to take my pills on an empty stomach so I decided that, not only would I fast from food, but I would also fast from taking my pills. I began to declare in the mirror every morning before I left my room "I am not A.D.D, Attention Deficit Disorder does not define me, my mind is whole in Christ Jesus." I went to class and walked around campus feeling so free and different. I couldn't remember the last time I intentionally woke up and didn't take my medicine. The fast ended and I had tests coming up the next week. Mentally I still wanted to stay off of my medicine but there was so much fear that my mind didn't measure up to everyone else's. With it being my first year in college, I felt like I needed to do well so I went back to taking my medicine, but every day that I took it I felt like a drag and I hated it.

Around the first week of October, I spoke to my older brother who had also been diagnosed with A.D.D. at a young age, but no longer was on any medication. I asked him what made him stop taking his medicine and his words to me were "I will either fail or succeed; but whatever I do will be of my own doing not the effect of ADD, the medicine, or the lack thereof." I truly admire my older brother and those words were so inspiring. I read his message and just sat there and meditated on it. I prayed that night that God would give me the strength to embrace who he truly created me to be. The Lord revealed to me that I was paralyzed by a fear of failure. I couldn't stand the thought of failing, to one day face that my worst fears were true and that maybe I really wasn't as good as everyone else. However, who we are is not based on a scale of how we perform compared to the world's performance but it's based on the greatness that God placed within us. That night I wrote the original decree that the Lord had given me and I stuck it to my mirror. The very next day I woke up, looked myself in the mirror, and declared that my mind was whole and that I was enough in God's eyes. I decided that I was going to step out on faith and that week I threw all of my pills away.

The rest of the year was a challenge that came with many internal conflicts and meltdowns where I questioned if I would be able to finish, if I was capable without my medicine. I decided to replace where I once took "booster pills for focus" with the word of God. When I got frustrated and I needed to study, I began to look up scriptures and seek God to fill in the gap for me. Scriptures such as James 1:5 says, *If any of you lack wisdom, let him ask of God, that giveth to all men liberally, and upbraideth not; and it shall be given him* and Deuteronomy 28:13 encouraged me that I was "the head and not the tail, above only and not beneath." The Word of God kept me focused better than a pill ever could. It was important that I not only broke free from the feeling that I was lacking, but I also renewed my mind to see what God truly placed inside of me. To remember that God is the creator and ultimate source of wisdom and we are created in his image! Being created in the image of God means that we have access to everything that he is. Once I accepted that I was made in his image, I had to go a step further to embrace it. I needed to believe that I am capable and not lacking anything.

Needless to say, it was not always easy but God brought me through. I finished my freshman year of college without any A.D.D. medicine and not only did I finish but I made the dean's list, ending the year with a grade point average of 3.57. It has now been three years of being completely medication free. The icing on the cake is that there is power in your testimony, not only did God use my brother to help me get free, but he then used my testimony to help another family member who was able to come off of his medication as well. I AM NOT A.D.D., and Attention Deficit Disorder DOES NOT DEFINE ME!

None Shall Be Barren
By: Gloria Golden

Lo, children are an heritage of the Lord: and the fruit of the womb is his reward. (Psalm 127:3)

    A warm sunny day in July 2008 brings forth a new little life. A precious little baby is born and my heart absolutely melts as I completely fall in love with this baby. "Too bad it's not my baby" I thought. That single thought; however, was a complete contradiction to my behavior and language up to that point in my life. I always said I didn't want to have any children. I didn't even like holding babies, but something was different about this baby. This child stirred up a feeling in me that I did not know existed and I did not want that feeling to pass. "I want to have a child" I thought to myself, and so I set out on what eventually became a three year emotional roller coaster.

    Before we even got engaged my husband shared his desire to have four children once he was married and I told him very clearly "I don't want children." He simply responded "ok" and did not push the issue. Since he responded so casually and never attempted to persuade me to feel differently I believed he respected my decision. After he proposed I thought to myself "this man truly loves me. He is willing to sacrifice having children and spend the rest of his life with me." Once we were married everyone we encountered would ask "when are you going to have kids and start a family?" My husband would always remain silent and let me answer the questions. Eventually, I dreaded hearing the question and giving people an answer. The first time I answered the question honestly and said "I don't want children" I was met with shock, disbelief and judgment. So I decided the next time someone asked me that question I would respond, but not necessarily answer their question. I gave responses like "we're just enjoying each other right now" and "we already started a family when we got married." I didn't know at the time that each thought, action and answer was cultivating the seed of doubt and helping it grow.

My husband and I had been married for almost two years when the desire to have children finally hit me. I rushed home and was so excited to share these new feelings with him. When I told him that I felt I was ready to have a baby he looked at me and smiled. He said very calmly, "I knew this day would come. The Lord told me that you would change your mind." At that moment I understood why he never pushed the issue in the past and why he never responded when people would ask us about having children. It was because he never stopped believing that he would have children with me; he didn't give up hope. Now that we both were in agreement about having a child I thought the hard part was behind us, but I could not have been more wrong.

Year One (2009 – 2010): Fertility Drugs

As I stated previously, this became a three year emotional roller coaster. Year one was full of trial and error as we worked on trying to have a child the natural way. Each month I waited with anticipation for my cycle "to not show up," but yet it still came. I was confused as to why I couldn't get pregnant so I made an appointment with my doctor. I told myself that I was pretty healthy and this checkup would confirm that thought. When arriving at the appointment and speaking to the doctor I explained I was ready to have a child and wanted an overall checkup to ensure things were fine, having seen no results. The doctor agreed to the checkup and also did some blood work. A few weeks later I received a phone call from the doctor's office asking me to come in for a follow up appointment. At the follow up, the doctor told me flat out that I did not ovulate regularly and would not be able to conceive a child without the assistance of fertility drugs. I sat there silent, in total shock. I was given a prescription for fertility drugs and told to follow up in a month. I left that office feeling defeated. I was a woman, yet I could not do the one thing that women should be able to do naturally – bare a child. Wiping away my tears I told my husband the outcome of the appointment and he said "this is your body so you do what feels right for you. I support whatever decision you make." I then filled the prescription because I thought that was my only option. After taking the fertility drugs for a few days I begin to experience excruciating pain on my side. It was almost debilitating. I was in so much pain that I was lashing out all the time and my desire for my husband nearly ceased. I told my husband I was going to stop the medication. I said "I do not want to keep using this medicine to force my body to do something that it should do naturally." I threw the medicine out that day.

Year Two (2010 – 2011): Health and Weight Problems

At the beginning of the following year I started experiencing some health related issues that put my conception plans on hold. I quickly made an appointment with my doctor to get a diagnosis and treatment so that I could get back to working on a child. The diagnosis was a simple bladder infection and after a few days of antibiotics I would be fine. However, when that infection went away I had another a few weeks later...then another and another. It was a horrible cycle of *infection-antibiotics-rest-repeat*. Frustrated that my doctor could not provide anything to eliminate the issue, I took matters into my own hands. I began researching my symptoms and found testimonials from others who experienced the same things I did and were now healed. After a little more digging I found the facility where they were treated and I made an appointment. During that appointment they ran various tests and took eight valves of blood to do a full food allergy assessment. A few weeks later I received all my test results. I was overweight, pre-diabetic, and I had a severe dairy allergy that was causing my chronic bladder infections. The doctor told me that if I wanted to have a child I needed to make some immediate changes health wise. I agreed and was paired with a dietician/nutritionist who helped me develop and maintain an eating plan to produce positive changes in my life. I began to feel that things were getting better and being able to have a child seemed much more attainable.

Year Three (2011 – 2012): Believe Only in the Word

Changing my lifestyle to become healthier had done wonders for my body. My weight was down, my blood sugar was normal and there were no more infections. Great, but why was I still not pregnant? I made all the right changes and in my mind those things should have worked enough for me to have gotten pregnant by now. Everyone around me seemed to be getting pregnant and I was finding it hard to be happy for them. Instead, I was envious of the fact that they were having babies and I was struggling. My husband and I received the news that another couple we knew was having a baby and I went in the bathroom and cried. When I came out my husband asked what was wrong and I confessed that I was angry and jealous that others were having kids instead of us. I even began to "justify" why I deserved a child and they didn't. I told him I didn't understand what we were doing wrong. He let me get it all out and hugged me and said "We're not doing anything wrong and it will be our time soon." I nodded in agreement, but couldn't shake the thought that it was not going to happen for us.

That Sunday while at church, the Pastor made a statement that hit me; I had an epiphany. He said, "Every word you speak is like a seed that you have planted in the ground. When you speak negatively or say something that contradicts that word it's like taking a shovel and digging that seed back up. Some of you are wondering why you have not received a harvest yet and it's because you dug up your seed with your words and your actions." I was blown away. For years I said I didn't want children and even after changing my mind I received blow after blow that it would not happen for us. For the past 2 years I had been cultivating the seeds of doubt and unbelief. I made the choice that day to believe that the Lord would bless us with a child when He was ready. The next day I went to work and created a vision board for us to have a child. *Write the vision and make it plain upon tables, that he may run that readeth it. For the vision is yet for an appointed time, but at the end it shall speak, and not lie: though it tarry, wait for it: because it will surely come, it will not tarry.* (Habakkuk 2:2-3) When I brought it home and showed it to my husband I told him "I'm done trying to do things my way. Children are a blessing from the Lord and I know He will give us a baby when the time is right." I hung the vision board up in my closet and said: "Lord, I'm giving this to you and I will no longer be stressed or anxious about having a child."

For the months that followed I continued to focus on my health and weight loss. I would look at the vision board in my closet on a daily basis and I believed that the Lord would allow that vision to come to pass. *Delight thyself also in the Lord: and he shall give thee the desires of thine heart.* (Psalm 37:4) He did so six months after creating that vision board. Around the time that my cycle was due, I started having some pre-cycle symptoms, but I was also really tired and having weird food cravings. That lasted for a few days and when my cycle didn't come I decided to take a home pregnancy test. While waiting for the results I had so many thoughts going through my mind, but I stayed focused on the scriptures in my vision. *Thou wilt keep him in perfect peace, whose mind is stayed on thee: because he trusteth in thee.* (Isaiah 26:3) When I looked down at the test and saw that it was positive I was stunned. I had been trying for two and a half years to have a baby and the Lord made it happen six months after I chose to completely give it over to him.

Telling my husband was one of the happiest moments of my life. I wrapped the test in a box and presented him with that gift. When he saw the positive test he cried tears of joy. That evening we prayed together, laid hands on my stomach and declared that I would have a full and blessed pregnancy with no sickness, issues or complications. *And none will miscarry or be barren in your land. I will give you a full life span.* (Exodus 23:26) Every word we spoke came to pass because we believed it would. In January 2013 I gave birth to a healthy baby boy. Holding him in my arms brought back the feeling that started me on this journey. This time, my feeling was stronger and more permanent. I felt love. It was different than the love I had for my husband or parents or siblings. It was the love that only a mother can have for her child. It's not always explainable, but it's true, it's deep, and it's unconditional.

Today, our family has grown to include another son and one little miracle that will debut in November 2018. The Lord has blessed us greatly with our children because that is the desire of His heart. *And he will love thee, and bless thee, and multiply thee: he will also bless the fruit of thy womb* (Deuteronomy 7:13).

Hope: Your Expectation For Tomorrow!
By: Minister Crystal L. Bradford

Why art thou cast down, O my soul? and why art thou disquieted within me? hope in God: for I shall yet praise him, who is the health of my countenance, and my God. – Psalm 43:5

I've often heard hope described as a place somewhere between present and future reality where the intangible things we desire aimlessly live….a place that's always future with no real direction to its destination. When we encounter someone in a difficult season of life, we say "I hope things work out," we encourage them by saying, 'don't lose hope'…there's always hope. This testimony is about the power of hope…but not the hope that I just described above. Hope is real!! Hope is not wishful thinking…it is a confident expectation. Hope is positioned right between faith and love. It is the faith that we have in God that allows us to have this type of hope! No matter what you are facing today, I pray this testimony will reignite the flame of hope that God has placed in you, remember…when all else is gone, hope remains!!

I pulled into my driveway from running a few early morning errands when my phone rang and I saw on the caller ID, it was the doctor's office. The week before, a large lump appeared on my neck, seemingly out of nowhere. I went to the emergency room and they referred me to an Ear, Nose and Throat (ENT) Specialist, who sent me to get a Computed Tomography (CT) scan. When I answered, the voice on the other end asked for me, when I acknowledged who I was she said: "Please hold on the doctor would like to speak to you." 1 Peter 4:7 is one of my life verses: *keep calm so you can pray*. Over the years, I have attempted to always make this my first response, so I took a deep breath and prayed for God to prepare me for whatever he was going to say. My previous experience caused immediate concern because doctors don't usually come speak with the patient; they convey whatever they need to say through their medical staff.

The doctor asked how I was feeling. He then went on to say that the radiologist reviewing my CT scan called him with concern. He said the words that you never want to hear your doctor say, "This doesn't look good." He went on to explain that he believed it to be Lymphoma. He wanted both my husband and I to come in the office first thing in the morning, so we could discuss a treatment plan. He then transferred me back to the receptionist to schedule the appointment.

I allowed my faith to lead me in a confession of what I already knew. The enemy had chosen to wage a war against me, he set his sight on my physical body. He launched a triple threat attack, beginning the previous year as I had begun to have some vision problems. The doctors weren't able to easily diagnose the disease because it didn't fit any of the usual parameters. After almost a year of specialist visits, intense testing and finally a trip to New York to see one last specialist, I was diagnosed with an advanced case of glaucoma. This diagnosis came in 2009. The following year, the enemy continued his attack in another area of my body. The diagnosis of Type 1 diabetes came in April of 2010. This attack had weakened me quite a bit and I knew that now the enemy thought he was about to launch his third and final attack to take me out, but God gave me a Word I made a decision to hold on to during the second attack. He told me that I was not to allow what I see to change what I know!! I took that Word from the Father as a command, not a suggestion. I wrote it everywhere to keep it before my eyes and this is how my faith grew as I meditated on this word. I knew there was evidence of God still working in my life! I knew that His promises were there for me to hold on to so I didn't slip away. It was the "now" faith that kept me going day by day. I knew that I wouldn't be able to get to the things I was hoping for if I didn't stay in the fight!! I couldn't quit. I had an expectation for tomorrow that I wasn't willing to let go in any way. It is the living hope that I have in Christ that gave me a solid foundation to stand on when things around me seemed to be falling down. In my daily prayer time I would speak aloud the things that I knew about God! I would reflect on his faithfulness, on the many times that He saved me in the past. I knew he would save me again!!

My friend Tammy and her husband came over and had already called our other friends, Larry and Tiffany. She told me we were going to meet at their house that evening to pray in preparation for the appointment the next day. Tammy said that she and her husband would go with us to the appointment to support us. I will never, ever forget the love and support that my friends showed towards me and my family that evening. They prepared dinner. We ate and then had a bible study about strongholds and deliverance. That evening, I received my first copy of <u>Prayers that Rout</u>

Demons by Apostle John Eckhardt. I went home being even more encouraged in my belief that I was going to get through this trial, that I am MORE than a conqueror! We went to the doctor the next morning as planned. It was great having our friends there with us. The doctor examined the mass while continually shaking his head and frowning his face. He performed a needle biopsy right there in the office but wanted to schedule for a full biopsy as soon as possible. When his staff contacted my primary care doctor for clearance for this surgery, she wanted to see me first.

Tammy and I made the drive to see my Primary Care doctor that afternoon. She said that this certainly had taken her off guard. I felt that I had to encourage her that everything was going to be ok. She said that she wanted to be sure that there were no other masses anywhere else so she ordered more scans. Over the next week I made at least three trips to the hospital for scans and bloodwork in preparation for this biopsy. That evening, we all met back at Larry and Tiffany's home to update everyone on the results of the day. We prayed again, we read more declarations. Larry and Tiffany instructed our family to come together daily to pray and to read the decrees from the book on healing. Our family chose to meet every day at 6:00p.m. We were still breaking out of the religious shell, by which we were so accustomed, and was practicing standing on the Word of God; so the family meeting time was very important. We had not been enlightened to the realm of healing that we were about to experience.

God knows each of his children and He provides perfectly for us. Late one evening, my dear friend Nneka called. She was aware of the diagnosis. She informed us that she had been praying and said, "I just need to come over and see this for myself...is it ok if I come over right now?" When she came, she read the doctors report and said, 'this is not so.' She looked at the lump, she touched it, she prayed and again said, 'this is not so.' We didn't even recognize the significance of her late night visit until some weeks later. She came around midnight and she declared that this is not so. What a powerful demonstration of her obedience to God and the blessing that we received through her. God does divinely order our days! The doctor was delayed in scheduling the biopsy due to the many other tests that needed to be completed coupled with his prior commitments. Approximately three weeks had passed and we went in for another office visit. The unusual symptoms had mostly disappeared and the lump wasn't as noticeable ...when we went in this time the doctor felt for the lump, he looked and then took a step back...he said, "It seems to be gone." He then sent me for a final scan to be sure that it was completely gone.

Through Christ, we received the victory! The lump left just as mysteriously as it had appeared! The enemy was defeated. There was no medication received for this, no radiation, no chemo...I never even had the full biopsy. There is no scar left from the lump....but what we do have is a priceless testimony!! God allowed the doctors, the medical staff, my co-workers and now you to benefit from this testimony. I pray that your hope is renewed! That whatever you are facing you will be renewed in your belief that God loves you!! I pray that you will allow His incredible love for you to be the cord that keeps you connected to hope! Hope... the bridge that connects the promise to the performance!

I have a living hope and this hope will not disappoint because it is an expression of His great love for me! What is my responsibility? To keep my mind stayed on Him! Don't get distracted by what it looks like. When we keep the proper perspective we don't lose hope! We understand that the Word of God is the Word of God, which he proclaims the end before the beginning and we will partake in all that he has for us. We cannot lose heart, we cannot grow weary! We must be aware of the times and the seasons as we stay anchored by hope, which becomes our expectation for tomorrow!!

By His Stripes I am Healed
By: Synesha Parish

Surely he hath borne our griefs, and carried our sorrows: yet we did esteem him stricken, smitten of God, and afflicted. But he was wounded for our transgressions, he was bruised for our iniquities: the chastisement of our peace was upon him; and with his stripes we are healed. (Isaiah 53: 4, 5)

By all accounts my life was great. I was married to a wonderful husband, a mother of five children with a loving family. I was a member of a great church, I had a good job, my own business, and a nice home. I married my best friend and we had been pushing through life together with our children. I was so grateful about all the things that God was doing in our lives. We were an active family and I truly enjoyed being with my children and doing fun things together as a family. My life was great!

This life that I had come to know changed drastically in 2012. I had recently lost 40 pounds gained during my last couple of pregnancies when one day, all of a sudden, I could not move my legs! I was in such tremendous, excruciating pain. I called out frantically for my husband! He came immediately to see why I was so distressed. I began to explain to him that I couldn't move my legs and was in pain. This was so bizarre and unusual and we just could not understand what was happening. This went on for a few hours but eventually I was able to walk again that evening, though it was a weird feeling.

I went on with life, not thinking too much about it again until the day my daughters were in the 4th of July Parade with their Girl Scout Troop and I joined the parents in walking the parade with our children. I remember walking at a normal pace until I began involuntarily walking slower. I remember noticing the rest of the parade being so far ahead of us. Before long I began to fall over on my daughter as the pain in my legs came back again and I could not walk. I tried to yell for help from anyone in the parade but I had fallen so far behind, the parade line was completely out of sight. I called my husband on the phone and he immediately came to pick us up from where we were and again, I could not fully understand what was happening.

Once I got home I decided to make some phone calls to set up appointments with doctors and specialists to find out what was happening with my body. I also began to pray and seek God for answers. My faith has always been strong and I knew that no matter the diagnosis, I was going to trust God. It took about one year of seeing many Doctors, Chiropractors, Holistic Doctors, Neurologists, Physical Therapists, and other Specialists and having many tests done to finally start getting answers. The doctors shared with me a litany of diagnosis in response to my symptoms that to my surprise was connected to my joints, hips, abdomen and pelvis.

They said that these types of injuries occur after multiple back-to-back births and can typically cause instability in the abdomen and pelvis. Although these challenges may have compromised my life physically, they did not compromise my spirit. I smiled through the pain and kept the joy of the

Lord in my heart as I was still so very grateful for life. I kept mediating on the scripture Isaiah 53: 4, 5. Even though I was in pain, I knew that by his stripes I was healed.

During this time, my body was very fragile and I could not walk more than 30 minutes at a time. I needed help doing even the smallest things like getting around the house and walking up the stairs. As much as I love to dance I was not able to do so during this time. I was told by the doctor not to lift heavy things, so it just broke my heart when I could not pick up my baby nor could my children sit on my lap. As a mother with small infant children, not being able to pick them up or hold them on my lap was emotionally painful. My body was always in a tremendous amount of pain. I tried to never let those around me or those who knew me personally know the level of pain I was experiencing because the Joy of the Lord and his love kept me going.

The scripture in Isaiah 41:10, reminds me that the Lord is my strength and no matter what it looks like, he would still get me through it. Regardless of the pain I was in, he still would see me through no matter how long it took to get answers. Even if I never get the answers I want, God would always be with me. I spoke Jeremiah 29:11 daily because I do believe his word, *For I know the thoughts that I think towards you, saith the Lord, thoughts of peace, and not of evil, to give you an expected end.* I may have continued increased pain, but I still believed God for my total healing.

This part of my journey has taught me so many things. The Lord continues to be faithful to His Word! In the past I could not walk longer than 30 minutes and today I have more days where I can walk longer than 30 minutes. In the past I could not walk up the stairs without help and today I walk up the stairs without assistance. There were many days throughout the week where I could not get out of the bed due to the level of pain I was in; however, today I can go weeks without having to stay in bed. Before, I could not dance due to the pain, but today there are many times where I have the ability to dance. All of this progress came from prayers, laying on of hands, deliverance and trusting God for my healing. I will continue to believe and trust God that my full and complete healing will come.

    I know in my spirit that God is in total and complete control and he is ordering my steps even in the midst of this journey. I know the Lord has healed me and wants me to keep moving and looking ahead no matter what the situation looks like because he is still my Father and healer! There are stories I've read about women with similar health challenges that have given up hope! I am here to tell you: "Don't give up!" The Lord does not want us to give up. I have not given up! I am moving forward, walking in my healing, trusting and believing that he has carried my sickness and borne my diseases and with his stripes I AM HEALED!

The Power of Prayer
Questions for Reflection/Discussion

1. Think about times in your life when your only recourse, solution or resolve was to pray for divine intervention. How did the Lord God intervene? What was the outcome?

2. Consider times when you tried to do things your way and not the Lord's. At what point did you give up and ask God for help? What happened?

3. Find biblical examples of how prayer changed the outcome of a situation. What is the difference between how the biblical character prayed and/or trusted God and how you typically pray and/or trust God?

4. Reflect on the situations where you could clearly see that the Lord answered your prayer. What was your behavior, thoughts or actions while waiting on the answer? What did you learn about yourself in the process? What did you learn about God?

5. Choose an author from this section of the book whose story resonates with you. Why is their story meaningful to you? How would you handle the situation if you were in their shoes?

The Power of Prayer: Questions for Reflection/Discussion

6. Write down the most pressing issue in your life. Why is this issue so important? What do you need God to do about it? What scripture(s) do you have to pray about it with power?

7. Are you ready/willing to pray according to the Word of God and watch Him move on your behalf? What are some hindrances to your prayer life? Are you willing to do what it takes to remove them?

8. Make a decision to improve the frequency and potency of your prayer life with the power of the Word of God.

We Don't Look Like What We've Been Through

PART II
LIVING LIFE ON PURPOSE

I recently asked a woman how she was doing and she replied, "I'm living my best life!!" This is currently the phrase of the season. Many people are purporting to live their "best life" by doing whatever it is that makes them happy. They mistakenly believe if they are doing what makes them happy, that is their best life. If we apply that logic to our lives, then most activities we deem sinful qualify us for our best life because in the moments of sinful glee, we are indeed happy. Drug addicts getting high are happy. Adulterers in the climax of a tryst, are happy. Folks getting a promotion by sabotaging co-workers are happy. Being momentarily, situationally or seasonally happy does not mean you are living your best life, especially if you are a Christian. Most Christians have the wrong idea about what it means to live their best life. I submit to you that living your best life is not: 1) Life without problems or issues 2) Getting everything you want from God or 3) Having everything you desire materially, relationally, financially, etc. The bible is very clear in Mark 8:36, *For what shall it profit a man, if he shall gain the whole world, and lose his own soul?*

Living your best life according to the Word of God is knowing you are sustained by the Father, *And God is able to make all grace abound toward you; that ye, always having all sufficiency in all things, may abound to every good work.* It's believing that you are more than a conqueror, *Nay, in all these things we are more than conquerors through him that loved us* (Romans 8:37). It's boldly proclaiming that you are an overcomer! *Who is he that overcometh the world, but he that believeth that Jesus is the Son of God* (1 John 5:5)? Living your best life in Christ is living life on purpose with the full backing, power, authority and protection of the Holy Ghost in the face of challenges, oppositions and trials. *But ye shall receive power, after that the Holy Ghost is come upon you: and ye shall be witnesses unto me both in Jerusalem, and in all Judaea, and in Samaria, and unto the uttermost part of the earth.* (Acts 1:8) *And we know that all things work together for good to them that love God, to them who are the called according to his purpose.* (Romans 8:28)

Part II is a Testament to what it looks like to live according to the purposes of God in spite of obstacles, failures, setbacks and tragedy. The women in this section testify to the power of God to move mountains, revive in the face of death, promote despite opposition, and succeed against all odds. What the authors have learned is, when you love God and are truly called according to His purpose, all things do work together for your good.

Listening To God and Finding Your Voice
By: Minister Quiana Kee

And Joshua said unto the children of Israel, How long are ye slack to go to possess the land, which the LORD God of your fathers hath given you? (Joshua 18:3)

    I haven't always felt comfortable asking for what I believe I deserve in my professional life. Insecurities about my worth and fear of rejection have hindered me from finding my voice. The enemy is cunning and crafty in that way. No matter how many times the voice of the Lord would tell me, "I will prosper you" or "This is what I have for you my child," I would still contend with the voice of the enemy. That cunning beast would say, "You're not good enough" or "Who do you think you are to ask for that?" I then began to adopt these messages as my own. There have been times in my career when I've allowed the voice of the enemy to overpower the voice of the Lord. Because of that, I've settled for whatever the world decided to give me.

    When I didn't get a promotion over the span of four years, I believed there was something I wasn't doing to receive it. Although I was working hard as an engineer, solving problems, and fulfilling a need at my company, I still didn't feel worthy enough to ask for a promotion. I didn't know how to say it or if I should say it. Being a double minority in a white, male-dominated company also didn't help. When I finally received the promotion, my manager began the conversation with "This is long overdue." I was so used to keeping my head down and putting in the work with the hope that someone would recognize me. I soon realized that this world would only give me what it wanted me to have and what I was willing to tolerate. This is defined as the bare minimum or less than God's best. Though the world is ruled by the prince of darkness who does not want me to prosper in a righteous way, it was by God's power and recognition that I received that promotion! Through the words of my manager, the Lord told me that the promotion had been available and set aside for me for some time. Why didn't I ask for it?

Later in my career, I decided to make the shift from engineering to project management. I wasn't satisfied with the way the project managers were leading the engineers. I felt that God could guide me to lead people in a better way -- in a way that serves others and helps them to excel in their work. God was changing my direction to lead others according to His Word. I became a Certified Project Manager and put my credentials on my resume. When my new manager saw my resume, he gave me a project to lead. I was excited to have the title of Project Manager! My boss had full confidence in my abilities and let me take the reins to lead a team of engineers. Even with that vote of confidence, I didn't broach the topic about salary or position grade because I chose to believe that I needed to prove myself worthy first (voice of the enemy, again). With three months under my belt in the new role, I began to wonder when my boss or HR would speak to me about a promotion or raise since my responsibilities had broadened significantly. Here I was again waiting for the world to recognize me and to acknowledge the fact that I was doing more for less. But God moved on my heart and gave me the words and the boldness to speak to my boss. During our conversation, I discovered that my Germany-based boss had no idea about my position grade or my salary in the US. Although HR had moved me under his responsibility, they didn't bother to change my position grade or even consider me for a salary increase. It wasn't a difficult discussion with my manager or a hard change for HR to advance my grade level and increase my salary. Again, the Lord had it ready for me. I just had to ask for it. Why didn't I ask for it sooner?

A few years later, I was working as a Senior Project Manager under a new boss. I had really hit my stride in my professional life! I was doing work that I enjoyed. I was helping my team do their best work and resolving issues for my customers. But when I received my annual raise, I heard the voice of the Lord say, "I have more for you." He was specifically speaking to me about my salary. I had no hard evidence about anyone else's salary being higher than mine, but the Lord told me that He had more for me than what I was receiving during the raise period. Over the following months, I wrestled with the idea of asking for more money from my company. Should I do it? What gives me the right to ask for more? Who do I think I am? What if they say no? All of these words were from the voice of the enemy -- messages of doubt, insecurity, and fear. Thankfully, my God had a stronger message for me in His Word. During my study time, He clearly asked me, "How long will you neglect to possess the land which I have given you?" (Joshua 18:3). How long was I going to allow doubt, insecurity, and fear to stand between me and His promises for me? As I walked through the halls of my building, God clearly showed me every project manager that was making six figures and I was not one of them. However, it wasn't shown to me in a way that would cause me to be covetous. God revealed it and let me know that what He had for me was even better than what the world was handing out. I had to remind myself to stop settling for bare the minimum and less than God's best -- GO and POSSESS IT!

God gave me the words to say to HR and to my manager about my salary. I asked them to do a "sanity check" on my salary in comparison to other Senior Project Managers with similar years of experience. After their review, they came back and said that I was indeed underpaid in comparison to others in my role. It wasn't the fault of my current manager that I was underpaid. God actually put him in position as my boss to help close the gap from previous times when I hesitated to ask for what God had for me. At that time, my boss had given me some of the highest bonuses and raises of my career. But even with that, there was still a gap when the salary review was completed. God's Word gave me boldness to overpower the voice of the enemy and to find my voice. My company adjusted my salary accordingly. I had finally possessed the land.

Now, as an executive with close to 20 years in my company, I have far less fear in asking for what I know the Lord has for me. Yes, I know -- it only took 20 years! His Word says, *Ask, and it shall be given you; seek, and ye shall find; knock, and it shall be opened unto you* (Matthew 7:7). When the executive position was offered to me, I did not hesitate to ask for more. I sought the Lord as well as wise counsel while drafting my counter-offer. The Lord told me not to accept what the world gives me. I was grateful for what was offered to me, but I humbly went before His throne knowing that He is able to do exceeding, abundantly above all that I could ask or think according to the power that works in me (Ephesians 3:20)! That power that works in me allowed me to counter with wisdom and boldness. As a result, I received more than the original offer! The power that works in me listens to God, silences the enemy, and helps me to find my voice according to God's Word.

Redefining Success
By: Suzanne Brockner

But Jesus beheld them, and said unto them, With men this is impossible; but with God all things are possible. (Matthew 19:26)

What is success? Is it making a lot of money? Is it being happy? Is it having a family? Is it freedom to do what you want? Is it being philanthropic? Is it momentary? Can it be permanent? Is success a feeling?

Let me share my thoughts and experiences on what success has been to me and who I am. I am a mother of a beautiful daughter who is married. I have a hearts' desire to hear God and please him in all I do and watch him work on my behalf. Singing worship songs is such a joy for me as I have been singing all my life. I earned a Master of Art's degree in Education and worked my way up the corporate ladder to middle management more than once. I have also been a professional real estate agent for several years, and have a strong entrepreneurial spirit. One could look at my life and say, "Wow, your life has been pretty successful! You've accomplished an awful lot!" That all sounds great, but there is more to this story.

While I experienced many successful moments, I also had some pretty tough blows that revealed my true heart and posture and reflected how much I really needed God. Although I had been a Christian all my life, I was only living it intermittently. I was a hearer of the word only and not a doer. I wasn't fully being a Christian, just merely demonstrating some Christ like qualities at times. I made decisions in my life that led me away from who I was, or who I wanted to become in life. Now the consequences of those decisions caused me to be depressed and feel defeated, like a failure. I needed to make some serious changes in my life.

My second-long term marriage was extremely damaging to me. But before I start there, let's go back to the beginning. When I was young, I wanted to figure things out for myself. I was very independent, goal driven and I had many dreams and aspirations with a strong drive to accomplish them all, but it took a while to get my priorities straight. I always had an internal longing to get married, have children, move up to a bigger house in a more expensive neighborhood, you know, have the American dream. I wanted a family, home, and security like any other woman; however, my life did not work out that way.

My dreams of having the family I wished for were delayed as I went to college and after graduation, immediately started working. I held many positions over the years as a teacher, a sales person but did not believe I could make money at what I really wanted to do for a career. I believed the lie that I would never be able to do what I loved and make a living doing it, so I continued to work hard at my current job. I worked fiercely, harder than any other of my co-workers and could not understand why they did not share the same work ethic. Eventually, I became a regional manager in the corporate world but that was not where I wanted to remain. I was so unsatisfied and unfulfilled in my work, level of earnings and lack of freedom with my time.

Then my biological clock started ticking louder and louder! My desire to have a baby was overwhelmingly strong. I got married, had a daughter, and then 10 years later I was divorced. I saw my husband through rose colored glasses and only saw what I wanted to see, not the truth of who he was in reality. We were not well suited. It was through that marriage that I learned to accept the truth about people and see things the way they are and not change things in my mind to make situations work out the way I think they should. God always knows what's best. Although the marriage didn't last, the most fulfilling moment in my life was when my daughter was born. It was pure joy being her Mom, loving her, raising her with a foundation of love and respect. What a gift! It was like walking into the light and staying there but being here on earth. It was during this time that I really began to give thanks and pray to God asking, talking, seeking and then most importantly, listening. It can be so hard to listen. I learned that in order to listen, I had to stop talking. Sound obvious, right?

Although I loved my husband, I did not like the Dr. Jekyll and Mr. Hyde act he portrayed daily. It reached a point where I knew I had to leave…with or without any of my things. I needed my peace back. As a result of all of the stress, I developed medical issues, lost all hope, and did not see a way out. But I did not want out of my marriage and I did not want to give up. I wanted it to be better. So I started listening. But, it still ended. It is amazing how many believers truly want to listen but are so busy figuring, thinking, talking, or complaining that they cannot receive. I came to understand that God is always talking to us. We just don't always hear. If we do hear, we don't always like what he's saying. Some of us actually will argue with God about what he is saying to us. Imagine that! Arguing with the maker of heaven and earth acting like we know better! I was a Christian all my life, but that does not mean I matured, internalized what that actually meant, or that my life was an accurate reflection of living the principals in the bible.

Four years after my divorce, I remarried. Although it lasted 17 years, I found myself divorced again. The damage from this marriage and subsequent divorce, as I mentioned, was extremely damaging to me. I learned the hard way that when something is wrong from the start, staying, praying and wanting it to be better does not make it better or fix what was wrong. This was such a painful and tough lesson that I did not learn the first time around. You see, if you need to learn a lesson in life, God will keep presenting the opportunity to you until you finally get it. I am probably not the only person who has had to learn the "hard way."

I made decisions in my life that lead me away from my true self. I came to the realization that I had to return to who I used to be and grow into the person that demonstrated God's love. Looking back at my decisions and how often I veered off the path there were very few boundaries. I allowed fear, doubt and worry to consume me at times. Any decisions made from that place lead me further away from whom I wanted to become. Looking back, the more mistakes I made, the more desperate I became inside and the more I saw myself as a failure. The truth is, I was not a failure. I was drawing that conclusion based on unhappiness at the time and what I was going through. Yes,

I understood that in Christ Jesus there is no condemnation. I knew God loved me. I believed the promises of God. I knew who I was in Christ Jesus and the authority, power and gifts that I received through the Holy Spirit. I just was not walking in them. Yes, there were times I did but not consistently. So, how do I get there? How do I get back to the person I was prior to allowing myself to be torn down. I had to now refocus my journey and work on how to get from where I am to where I was before the detours of life. I read many books to transform my mind on the subject.

    I finally figured out that success is what happens after you humbly believe in yourself, consistently take action to meet your goals, and reject the lies that come into your head. Success comes when you weather the ups and downs, persevere no matter what comes your way and never give up. For me, success was moving the mountain. A mountain is something that is standing in my way and blocking my ability to be successful. Learning how to move the mountain took me on a long journey. It involved shifting my priorities, desires, habits, way of thinking, and my inner dialogue with myself. I now have a full knowledge of and have gained a rock solid understanding of who I am. Matthew 17:20 took on a new meaning for me. It says: *Because you have so little faith. Truly I tell you, if you have faith as small as a mustard seed, you can say to this mountain, move from here to there, and it will move. Nothing will be impossible for you.* That is a strong scripture. It took me years to understand this scripture and really internalize it. In Matthew 19:26, Jesus looked at them and said, *with man this is impossible, but with God all things are possible.* All things? Wow! That gave me hope! My faith and belief in Christ Jesus had to come first. Doing life myself did not bring me peace or inner happiness. There was always something missing. I made missteps and at times pride ran high. I was not giving credit to my maker but to myself for my accomplishments. A friend once asked me, "Who are you serving first?" I had the order mixed up. I would have sustainable success if I served God first instead of second. I learned another valuable lesson. Don't try to do it alone! Put God first, give Him the glory, thanks, and all of the credit. Humility did not come easy for me in the early days.

    I continued to work on me and realized that I needed to set more boundaries. Everything I needed to be successful I already possessed. I had gifts, talents, abilities, intelligence and a relentless spirit. But I still felt I was all over the place and needed to focus. I had a hard time saying no to people because as a people pleaser, I did not want to disappoint anyone. God was teaching me to set boundaries with others by my actions and what I say. The scriptures say that the power of life and death are in the tongue (Proverbs 18:21). The tongue speaks what's in our hearts and our thoughts and we have a choice in what we choose to say. I began to speak the bad thoughts about myself and others because that was in my heart. I allowed my thoughts to control me. But we control our thoughts. Our thoughts do not have to control us, unless we allow it. There are two forces in this world, good and evil, and they are constantly at war. I decided I was not going to allow evil to win any longer. The devil comes to kill, steal and destroy. If we are not careful, evil can begin to manifest in our thoughts and minds. The enemy of our souls can begin to quietly whisper lies to us about ourselves with the intention of stopping us from becoming what God created us to be in Him. I finally made a decision that I would no longer be doomed by those bad thoughts and understood that they were not truths but lies! What a relief! Wow! I was on the road to Success. I understood another key thing I needed to change. I did not have to spend a second thinking about the lies!

Once I understood these key principles and began working on being a better Christian, putting God first, setting boundaries, and controlling my thoughts, I could clearly see the true definition of Success. Success is living the dream: Doing what I love, flowing in God's abundance and blessing others. Doing these things was not work to me. I refused to succumb to society's idea that says doing work to get ahead will open the door to your future.

Success is walking in peace, joy, and love. When I began to do this doors opened and prosperity flowed. I was happy, fulfilled, and full of love for God, myself and others.

Never stop learning. Stay young at heart. Never stop dreaming. Always believe.

Preparation Opens the Door for God's Manifestation
By: Brianna Bradford

I have planted, Apollos watered; but God gave the increase. (I Corinthians 3:6)

In business we say that success is when opportunity and preparation meet. In 1 Corinthians 3:6, Paul says, "I planted, Apollos watered; but God gave the increase." If you want success, God's way, you must prepare by planting the seeds He gives, watering that seed until it grows and then opportunity will manifest. This testimony is an example of God's success through me. First let me give you some background…

In February of 2018 I began reading this book called: <u>Prophetic Evangelism Made Simple – Prophetic Seed Sowing</u> by Matthew Robert Payne. This book was recommended to me by my Apostle because I expressed an interest in learning more about the prophetic. Typically it takes me a while to get through a book because I will start the book and then get distracted with other things and then pick the book up again months later. This was not the case this time, I was committed. I decided that I was going to read a few chapters each night before bed, and I was going to follow through this time! There was something special about this book and I felt that God was calling me to NOT delay. Wow! Talk about eye opening! As I read the book I began to see areas in my life (opportunities) where I could have prophesied to others.

At the same time, I was also preparing for a trip that I booked over a year earlier with one of my friends from college. We booked a trip through a travel agency with a group of about 12 young diverse people (whom we did not know) to Italy! The special thing about this travel agency is that you are given a "tour guide" who is familiar with the area and who will be with you along the trip. This wasn't my first time out of the country but every time I prepare to leave my home for a trip I become anxiously excited. To calm my "anxious excitement" I began speaking to God about it. As we talked, my prayer was that God would allow me, in whatever way, to be a light in the darkness. I don't like being outside my comfort zone and this trip was far out of that zone!

Now back to the book I was reading. About half way through the month of March I finished the book! The last chapter in the book is titled "practice makes perfect" and as you can guess by the title it was encouraging us as the readers to begin practicing to prophesy, specifically applying some of the new techniques from the book. This book was teaching prophecy from the perspective of prophesying to people we do not know for the purpose of evangelism. Prior to reading the book I've had experience with prophesying to my friends and family but not to people I did not know. So I pushed myself to be intentional during my prayer time to ask God for a prophetic word for my friends and it went well. I was becoming more comfortable with prophesying every day. I even began to receive prophetic words at times that I wasn't initially praying for them!

Preparation Opens the Door for God's Manifestation

It was now April and I was packed and ready for my trip to Italy! (I was physically packed and I prepared myself mentally for the journey ahead.) During day two of the trip our group was split into two cars as we traveled up the mountain for the day's excursion. During our climb up the mountain the people in our car began to have a conversation of sorts with the youngest person on our trip. We were all trying to give this young man advice about his life, college, relationships, religion etc. Given that this was only day two of our trip it was clear that we all probably confused him rather than helped him because of all the varying opinions that we each expressed. Nonetheless, it was to be expected in a car of mostly strangers who just the day before, met each other for the first time. It was during this conversation I had to exercise some self-control and patience as I heard others giving this young man advice that I knew in my spirit was not the way he should go! During my Morning Prayer time on the third day, I made sure to include the young man in my prayers and to my surprise (don't know why I was surprised) God gave me a word for him. So I made a note in my phone with the prophetic word that God gave me for the young man. Now, let me remind you that prior to this I've only had practice prophesying to people that I know like my friends and family. So I was going to need some time for God to reveal to me how I should go about delivering this word to the young man. I have to admit I was a bit nervous…I was thinking, why would this young man desire to hear from a stranger whom he just met?

On day four of our trip we had a free day to relax and explore the area on our own. During the day, my friend and I decided to do a little more relaxing than exploring. During my time of relaxation I went to watch television on my phone but the internet was not working properly so I ended up reading a book that I packed. The book was called <u>Wholeness: Winning in Life from the Inside Out</u> by Toure' Roberts. As I was reading this book, God began to remind me of the word that he gave me for the young man. So, as good as this book was, I had to put it aside to focus on this prophetic word again, specifically the delivery of this word. As I was thinking about it, I remembered that we created a group chat so that we could more easily get in contact with one another on the trip. This is when my overthinking nature began to set in…What if he doesn't respond? I had to cast down this thought and step out on faith. I had to remind myself that this was not about Brianna but this was about helping this man receive the Word of God.

Typically with my friends and family I would text them the prophetic word starting with, "Hey… I'm reaching out because God placed this word on my heart to share with you," and then I would proceed with the word. But this time was different; I remembered that there is this thing called the threshold principle I learned from bible study. This principle basically says that there is a "threshold" line that I must ask to cross or ask to be invited in before I could share a prayer or prophetic word with a stranger. So instead of texting the word I just simply sent him a text stating that I prayed for him and God placed a word on my heart for him, then I asked if he minded if I shared it. His response was "Please do!" and that we could talk later that evening when the group got together to hangout. I was excited of course, but also nervous because I had never done this before, so I had to prepare myself. I prayed, asking God to give me the right words to say during this conversation. I asked God to prepare him so that he would be able to receive and that God would remove all anxiety from me so I could deliver His right now word to his beloved son. When the time came to hang out with the group the young man ended up playing cards the entire evening so we didn't get a chance to speak about the prophetic word.

WOMP WOMP! I was a bit disappointed, but I was not going to give up this easily!

When I returned home that evening from the hangout I sent him a message and asked him if he wanted to talk over breakfast the next morning. Morning came and there was no response. So I went on with my day. The following evening after dinner I was reading my book when God reminded me again that I still needed to deliver this word. So I sent another message, this time I asked if he wanted me to just text him what I was going to say. He responded and said he hadn't seen the other message until later in the day but he still wanted to meet up if possible but it was up to me. Up to me right? If it was up to me I would have just sent the text but I knew it was actually up to God and God said that it should be delivered in person.

So I met with the young man; we talked, I explained to him what a prophetic word is, I shared the word I had received for him, we talked some more and as we were talking I received another prophetic word that I shared with him. As I shared the second prophetic word with him, he began to cry and I could tell that "IT" was happening. At this moment I could literally feel the presence of God. All of the anxiety and pressure I felt up to this point suddenly subsided. We were sitting outside on a ledge on this calm Italian evening and my heart was so full! God was touching this young man in a way that only God can do and this young man was able to feel the peace, love, and comfort of the Holy Spirit through me! It was an amazing experience because that evening this young man's life was changed through one word.

The next day was our final day together and after our final group dinner we ended the evening with some words of wisdom from our "tour guide." He began telling us that this trip to Italy was only the beginning that every one of us was in a season of transition in our lives. His exact words were "This is just a seed" for our future and we needed to continue to let this seed grow. There were some things that each of us needed to do in our lives to change and adapt to this transition (little did he know but these were some of the same words that God gave me for the young man.) I looked over and the young man just smiled at me because he heard it too. If you remember from the beginning of this testimony, the book that started me off on this journey was about prophetic <u>seed</u> sowing.

Traveling across the world to Italy was wonderful; the food, the people and the culture. But I must say that the climax of this trip I will never forget was the day God spoke through me to impart a prophetic seed into this young man's life. Out of all the people in the world, he chose me to hand deliver a word to this young man. Wow! Let me remind you that God is always working to prepare you for the next thing and although we don't always know what that next thing may be, we must be willing to put in the work that is required to be prepared. Remember; success is when preparation and opportunity meet. If you aren't prepared when the opportunity comes, it won't end in success.

Raising the Bar
By: Prophet Tiffany L. Henderson

And though the Lord give you the bread of adversity, and the water of affliction, yet shall not thy teachers be removed into a corner any more, but thine eyes shall see thy teachers: And thine ears shall hear a word behind thee, saying, This is the way, walk ye in it, when ye turn to the right hand, and when ye turn to the left. (Isaiah 30: 20, 21)

Matlock, Perry Mason, and Johnnie Cochran are all famous attorneys (fictional and real) that inspired me to become a lawyer. I wanted to go into a courtroom, wow a jury and win! I saw myself doing this as a little girl and held on to that dream from childhood into college. When I arrived at Howard University, I was gung ho and excited to take on the world! I was so resolute about becoming an attorney that I took a legal writing course in my second semester. By the end of that semester I was so disenchanted by the law, overwhelmed by the work and writing involved, that I decided the legal profession was not for me. I gave up on my dreams after one semester (on the undergraduate level) and one class. Terrible!!

I eventually transferred schools, got married in my senior year of college and graduated not even thinking about becoming an attorney. After college, I worked in the financial aid office of my school while my husband finished his engineering degree. While walking down the street on my lunch break I saw a billboard that read, "God Allows U-Turns." I stopped dead in my tracks. I read and reread the sign contemplating my life's decisions. God allows U-Turns? Wow! I kept walking and thinking, "Do I need to U-Turn?" As a matter of fact, the message of the billboard never left me.

When my husband and I moved to Illinois for his job in engineering, I became pregnant not long thereafter. Pregnant and unemployed with no career in sight, I became frustrated. How can I bring this child into the world and have no legacy to leave them? I felt as if I would do this child a huge disservice if I did not have a career or life worth looking up to for my first born. I began to think about my rash decision to not pursue a legal career and wondered, "Have I missed my opportunity to go to law school? Are my dreams of becoming a lawyer dead and gone?"

It was in these moments of frustration that the Lord reminded me of the billboard. "I allow U-Turns Tiffany! Go back to your first love, the passion I placed inside you from childhood! It was me (The Lord Your God) that gave you the desire to be a lawyer for my purpose!" It was then that I made the decision to go to law school. I applied to three different law schools and was accepted into all three! I decided early on that I would go to the school that gave me the most money. I received a Full Scholarship plus a monthly stipend! Hallelujah! The Lord truly wanted me to go to law school! He paved the way and paid in full!!

Our first child was only five months old when I started law school. By the grace of God I made it through all three years of law school. My celebration of graduation was short lived. It was now time to study for the "infamous" Bar Exam. I signed up for three different bar review study courses. In my mind, I had one shot at passing the bar with a three year old and a family who needed a second income! At this same time, my husband began working on his MBA so we really needed me to work! I began taking the study courses, studying with groups and on my own for 15-18 hours a day. I was determined to pass the first time.

With each study course, they provide practice exams. I took my first practice exam and failed miserably. I didn't panic because I'd just begun studying and knew I had a long way to go. I continued to study, went to review class and studied with others. I then took a practice exam every week and every week I would fail the exam. After about a month of studying (with only a few weeks left before the exam) I broke down. I cried like a baby. How could I have come so far through this process just to fail? I couldn't believe how little I understood and why I could not answer the questions correctly. Frustrated, stressed and tired, I cried for the rest of the day and temporarily gave up studying. Once I stopped crying, I prayed. "Lord where am I going wrong? What will it take for me to pass this test? I know you didn't bring me this far to leave me, so what am I supposed to do?" The Lord began to encourage me to trust Him. He said, "Your answers are in my Word. Don't stop studying my Word while you pursue what I have for you!" Admittedly, I was not studying my Word or praying like I should during this time. I was so concerned about not studying enough for the bar, I neglected the Word of God. I took the entire day praying and studying God's Word. During this time of prayer and studying, the Lord led me to the one passage that would be my saving grace:

And though the Lord give you the bread of adversity, and the water of affliction, yet shall not thy teachers be removed into a corner any more, but thine eyes shall see thy teachers: and thine ears shall hear a word behind thee, saying, This is the way, walk ye in it, when ye turn to the right hand, and when ye turn to the left. (Isaiah 30: 20, 21)

Oh My Goodness!!! When I tell you I had not received a more relevant word in all my life, I'm telling you the truth! I had been eating adversity and drinking affliction at every turn studying for this exam! I had no idea the worst had yet to be revealed.

From that day forward, I started my day speaking this Word. "My teachers will not be in a corner, but I will see my teachers and I will hear a Word behind me saying, this is the way, walk ye in it!" I began to build up myself on my most Holy faith praying in the Holy Ghost and declaring this Word over my life. I continued studying alone, in groups and in class. I then took my first practice exam after changing my methods and studying the Word… and I failed again. I almost passed out! How could I still fail after this? I thought the Lord was going to help me? Nevertheless, I continued on. I got over myself and continued to believe God and take Him at His Word.

The week before the exam tragedy struck our family. My husband's grandmother passed away in Ohio. He was devastated and distraught. I then had to encourage him through one of the toughest moments of his life. We went to Ohio to help his mother make arrangements and take care of his grandmothers' estate. My husband drove me back home the day before the exam, which was also the day before the funeral, and he had to give the eulogy.

Sitting for the exam, I sat with my test in front of me with mixed emotions. Up until that point, I still had not passed a practice exam and I was truly concerned about my husband's state of mind while he eulogized and buried the woman who kept him as a child and positioned him to receive Christ. I had much to overcome to pass this exam. I knew that the only way I could pass would be if the Lord literally gave me the answers. I opened the test booklet and immediately began making my declarations speaking Isaiah 30:20, 21. I went question by question: "Lord you said I would see my teachers and hear a word behind me saying this is the way walk in it. What's the answer?" I would then hear, A, or B, or C, etc. I took my time and quite literally asked the Lord for every answer!

A few months later I got my results back and passed the bar the first time! I was so excited! I screamed and shouted so much throughout the house that my then three year old son asked me what was wrong! I said, "I passed the bar! I passed the bar!" He immediately began jumping and shouting with me saying, "We passed the bar! We passed the bar!" My son could not fully appreciate what was happening, but he knew to rejoice because I was rejoicing!

The bible says, *For we walk by faith, not by sight* (2 Cor. 5:7). I could not see how I was going to pass one of the biggest tests of my life and the Lord had to show me through faith. I am now a practicing attorney for over 12 years! This profession has been a very pivotal key to opening many strategic doors in my life, the life of my family and my church. It was certainly God's will for me to be a lawyer all those years ago which is why he took me through a process of raising the bar of faith in my life to actually pass the bar exam and live out His purpose for me!!

College Changes Everything
By: Kimberly Shaw

Behold, I will do a new thing; now it shall spring forth; shall ye not know it? I will even make a way in the wilderness, and rivers in the desert. (Isaiah 43:19)

Academically, I struggled in high school. I don't think I got an "A" in any of my academic classes my whole high school career. Freshman and sophomore year, I really tried. I studied, went to get extra help, made sure I did all of my homework, but could never end the semester with an "A" in any academic class. By my junior year I stopped trying. I began to believe in my mind that I was not a smart girl, so school became less of a priority for me. I eventually became disengaged in all my classes, falling asleep and eventually I started skipping class. I knew what classes I needed to graduate and the rest was a waste of time in my mind. I never intended to be a scholar anyway so I did what I needed to do to get out and move on in life.

Second semester of senior year the main topic of conversation among my peers was college. Everyone was asking, what school are you going to? What's your major? I was even talking with a good friend of mine and she began to tell me about her college plans when she asked me, "Kim, what are your college plans?" I gave her this look of confusion. I couldn't understand why she would even ask me that question. She doesn't know I'm not college material? I wasn't an honor student like she was so, what made her think I even had college plans? I finally answered and said, "Girl, I'm not going to college. I'm done with school the moment I walk across the stage." I didn't have a plan for what I was doing instead of going to college, I just knew I wasn't going. College wasn't for people like me, it was for smart people who liked school.

The summer after graduation is the time I like to refer to as the "Summer of Freedom." I planned to live my best life from that moment on without school. All I wanted to do was work and be grown. About half way through the summer my mom began to question me about my plans for my life. Apparently, working at Aeropostale with my 30 percent discount did not qualify me as grown. She gave me the ultimatum that saved my life. She said, "You either need to find a full-time job or go to school, but working that little retail job is not enough." I remember feeling really frustrated, nervous and confused. Frustrated because I really thought I was done with school forever, nervous because I had not done anything to prepare for college and confused because I didn't know the first thing about getting into college. The only thing I knew to do was go to the community college. I heard that everyone gets into community college, so the next morning I walked up to the school and began my journey.

When I said I was confused about college I meant that! I didn't even know which door to walk through once I got to the school. I followed a girl inside who was carrying a folder in her hand. I thought maybe we'd be going the same way, maybe she was here to "register" for college too. Once I got inside there was a long hallway with random offices to the left and right. As I followed this girl down the hall, in the very first office on the right I heard someone say something about seeing an admissions counselor to start classes. I stopped in my tracks and thought, this might be the office I need. I walked in, marched right up to the desk and said, "Hi, I'd like to register myself for college." The receptionist gave me a strange look and said, "Do you mean register for classes?" I said 'sure.' She then told me that if I needed to register for classes I needed to go down to the end of the hall and to the left to the office of registration. So that's what I did. Once I got to registration I said again, "Hello, I'd like to register for college." This receptionist gave me the same strange look and said "Do you mean register for classes?" I said, "Yes, I guess that's what it is." She asked me what classes I needed to register for and now I was the one with the confused look on my face. I had no idea what classes I needed. Wasn't that her job? I told her I didn't know what classes to take I was just here to get registered. She then told me I needed to see an Academic Counselor and that they would help me find some classes. She said I needed to go back up the hall to the first door on the left for the Counseling Center. So that's what I did.

Once I got there, I walked in and this time I said, "Hello, I'd like to see a counselor, so I can register for classes." She said, "Well, you wouldn't register here, you'd register with registration." I told her I already went there and they told me to come to this office because I don't have any classes. She then had me sign in to see a counselor. About ten minutes later I was meeting with a counselor only to find out I couldn't get any classes because I didn't have any records at the school. I didn't have any records because I never applied. Then, I was sent back to the admissions office where I started. At that point I was ready to cry because I was so frustrated. I had been at that school for an hour walking from office to office standing in line after line only to end up right where I started. All I wanted to do was go home and tell my mom that I'd rather go to work because if it was this hard to get into college I can only imagine how hard it would be to take classes.

    As I walked back down the hall to the Admissions office I was having a real conversation with myself. I really didn't know what I was thinking trying to go to college. I had no idea what I was doing, people like me don't go to college, I should just go home, I thought. I reached the end of the hall and I stood there thinking, I could either keep walking out this door or give this one more try to see if I could get some help. Since I'm already here, I may as well see if could get some help. I walked back into the admissions office and asked, "Can I please see an admissions counselor? I'd like to apply for college." The receptionist looked at me because she knew I had been there earlier and said, "Oh, ok, sure please sign in and someone will be right with you." After waiting about five minutes the admissions counselor came out to greet me and took me back to her office. As soon as I sat down, I released all my frustrations and emotions out to her. She smiled and said, "Don't worry, I will help you. I will make sure you have everything you need before you leave."

    The admissions counselor helped me tremendously by putting me on the right path. The only thing I needed to do was get my financial aid together. She warned me that because it was so late in the summer I may have a hard time getting everything done in time but to try anyway. I walked into the office and told the receptionist I needed to fill out my financial aid. She handed me a paper form and told me to complete it and bring it back when it was done. I sat down, and the only question I could answer was my name and address. Everything else seemed like it was in another language. I panicked and left. This was too much to handle in one day.

I went home and told my mom what happened with the financial aid and asked for her help. She told me the only thing she knew to do was give me her tax information since that's what she did for my brother. She had no idea what to do after that. So, I called my brother and asked him if he knew what to do. He made a phone call and then told me it's better to have a professional help. He told me to go back to the financial aid office again the next day and ask to see his friend and he would help me. I got to the school and saw my brother's friend. He was very helpful and nice and told me it would be a few weeks before everything would go through.

The first day of school came and I was at school ready to start. I went to my first class and realized I was missing one very important thing. My BOOKS!! Where did everyone get their books? Was I late and missed it when the instructor handed them out? I asked the girl next to me where she got her book. She said she picked them up from the bookstore downstairs. I looked at her with the most disgusted look and said "So you bought this?" She said "Yes, I bought all of my books. Did you order yours or something?" I was so confused (yet again). I thought I had everything figured out. I didn't know you had to buy your own books! No one told me I had to buy my own books! I looked and said "No, I didn't buy them yet maybe I'll get them after class. How much are they here?" She said, "Well this one was $175 and was the cheapest. My others were really expensive." I could have died. Where was I going to get that kind of money? I told her "Oh, I might not have any books then because I don't have that kind of money." She said "Oh girl, me either! I used my financial aid." Oh yea, financial aid! I had forgotten all about that. So after class, I went down to the office and asked if I could use my financial aid to buy my books. The receptionist told me my financial aid was not processed yet. She told me I was doing everything very close to the deadline and that I might want to think about paying out of pocket and being reimbursed once my financial aid is done. Once again, I was frustrated that this college thing was becoming the worst decision I ever made. I was so frustrated I took everything out on the receptionist. After she sat there and listened to me, she sent me to see another counselor, this time a woman. She worked with me to make sure I understood what was going on and that I had what I needed to get my books.

The process I went through was exactly what I needed to fully appreciate what I do for a career now. The college process can be very confusing for anyone, especially someone who knows nothing about how it works. I didn't know the first thing about college, let alone how to enroll. The truth is, I was really late in getting everything done for school. The Lord showed me much grace by adding people in my path who were willing to help me. Looking back, I see why I have such a passion for helping people with this process. I didn't have anyone to hold my hand through this process; at least I didn't think I did. I now know it was the Lord speaking through my mom and forcing me to make a choice about my future. It was the Lord who prodded me to go into that office a second time when I could have gone home. It was him who made sure I talked with people who wanted to help me. Through this, Jesus has now put me in a position to be that person to help those confused, lost and frustrated students. Every student who comes into my office flustered because of what they've been through trying to navigate their way through this process, makes me smile because I know they were sent to me for a reason. It's now my chance to allow God to work through me. My co-workers in the past have told me I do too much for my students, but I know otherwise. I know I was put here for a reason. The patience I have for students and their parents come from the fire and desire inside me to help them succeed when they want to give up.

Once I became a college student I became very fascinated by the college process. I felt like everyone should have an education. I wanted and needed to know everything about the process so I could help everyone who was just like me. Little did I know, that was the start of my career. I started out as a work-study student in all of the student service offices at the community college, where I learned how a college functions. I spent the most time working in the Financial Aid Office as a Financial Aid Peer Mentor helping students complete their FAFSA. I later went on to Northern Illinois University where I became the president of a mentoring program that helped freshman and sophomore students get adjusted to college. After College, I worked for the state of Illinois as an Outreach worker helping students and their families' complete FAFSA applications and conducted workshops on financial aid. Now, I am a Financial Aid Counselor at Roosevelt University.

Though it may seem like financial aid is the career path for me the Lord has much more in store. I am the Education Ambassador for the Seven Mountain Council at the Kingdom Advancement Center and the Scholarship

Director where it is my job to help students go from high school to college and into their God given careers. We never know what God has in store for us on the other end of our college education. So, if the Lord has been moving you toward that direction, don't be afraid to do it. College is for everyone who wants to be educated at the collegiate level. I never saw this coming as an unmotivated high school senior who thought living her best life was a life without a college education. I thank God for the push in another direction because, college really did change everything for me.

Workplace Miracles
By: Shelia Roberts

And even to your old age I am he; and even to hoar hairs will I carry you: I have made, and I will bear; even I will carry, and will deliver you. (Isaiah 46:4)

The alarm clock went off and it was time to go to work. It seemed as though I had just gone to sleep. I worked at the hospital from 4:00 pm until 11:30 pm the night before. This was after working my shift from 7:00 am to 3:30 pm at my second hospital job. It had been a sixteen-hour day. Now, I was getting up to work a 12 hour shift again at the second hospital. I was working extra hours to help my daughter finish law school. My head hurt so badly, but I knew that calling off was not an option. I had to get through the day. I had the next day off and a doctor's appointment to address the ongoing headaches.

The next day at the appointment, the doctor's diagnosis was a simple sinus infection. The treatment would be a course of antibiotics for the next ten days. This was good I thought, I would feel better in twenty-four hours. I got over that infection just in time to be re-infected with another and then another. Soon my chest was congested. This meant more trips to the doctor and more antibiotics to clear the chest! It was a vicious cycle and I was both sick and tired.

After a grueling eight hours down and four more to go, this particular day, I was feeling really bad. I was sitting at the nurses station charting, when someone walked up and said "Hi Sheila, how are you?" and I lost it. I said, "I am so sick! It's been going on for so long and I am not getting any better. I don't think that I can take it anymore." I know that it was divine timing and positioning that one of the Pulmonary Specialists walked up and wanted to know why I was crying. The nurses explained what had been going on with me. He came around the counter, gave me a hug and said, "Stop crying, call my office and make an appointment to see me."

I followed his instructions and made an appointment with his office even though I was unsure if I could afford it. After my initial exam, he ordered a very expensive diagnostic test called a Pulmonary Function Test. As a result of the test I was diagnosed with asthma and given several medications and an inhaler to start treatment. The Pulmonary Specialist was part of a medical group and all the services rendered by his office were billable. He graciously paid it all for me!! *And my God will meet all your needs according to his glorious riches in Christ Jesus.* (Philippians 4:19)

During the time of my medical issues, I was the lead respiratory therapist in the Critical Care Unit (CCU) at my first hospital. I was responsible for taking care of critically ill patients, many whom were on life support systems. For some of those patients, I was not just a respiratory therapist, but a confidant and prayer partner during their time of need. Regardless of what I was experiencing personally, the Lord used me mightily at my job. The following, are some of the significant examples that have shaped my belief and increased my faith over the years:

Once, there was a famous celebrity impersonator who was on his death bed. The doctors gave up hope and called the family in to prepare them for the worse. The family came, but they had not given up hope. They began praying and only allowed in nurses that believed. As a believer I was allowed in to pray with the family. Thanks to those prayers he recovered, walked out of the hospital and continued performing.

There was a young lady that was on a ventilator with major complications after undergoing gastric bypass surgery. The Lord kept speaking to me saying, "Go pray for her!" I could feel the presence of the Lord upon me. I told her mother, "Your daughter is not going to die. She will live and proclaim the works of the Lord." Her mother asked, "Did the Lord say that to you?" I told her "Yes." The young lady recovered completely and walked out of the hospital.

A woman came in with a cancer diagnosis. She was very distraught and didn't want her kids to know, so she pushed them away trying not to burden them. I told her how 30 years ago I was diagnosed with dysplasia (a precursor to cervical cancer) and after receiving my diagnosis I sat in my car and thanked the Lord for giving me three girls. I always wanted children and prayed for them in my youth and God blessed me. I told her how grateful I was to God for giving me children and urged her to be grateful also and allow her kids to love her as well. She reconciled with her children before she passed away two weeks later.

One patient was transitioning to die. The doctor's said there was nothing more they could do, but his children prayed without ceasing. That patient made a full recovery and was able to walk out of the hospital, but turned around to walk back in to say thank you. He was not the only patient to do this. Many people came back and thanked me for praying with them and helping them when they were ill.

Not everyone viewed me the way these patients did. There were some people who absolutely did not like me and attempted on several occasions to set me up for failure.

As I mentioned before I was a Respiratory Therapist in the Critical Care Unit (CCU). There was an education coordinator, I will call him Ray, who had a huge problem with me. He hated that I held the position that I did and how the patients responded to me. Shortly after he was hired, on two separate occasions, he hired one of his friends, and pulled me out of my unit to replace me with his buddy. These friends were reputed to be outstanding clinicians; however they made major mistakes with patients and I was called in to correct their problems. Because I established a good rapport with the doctors and the nurses, they considered hiring me away from the respiratory department to be their staff therapist. This would prevent me from having to leave the unit again. Unfortunately, things could not be done this way. Ray, in his supervisory position, came to talk to me one day. He told me that the Director asked him to speak to me because there were several complaints about me from my coworkers. The complaint was that "I had gotten too big for my britches." I refused to talk to him and asked to speak to the Director personally. Of course Ray refused my request, so I called the Director myself and was invited to his office. When I got there Ray was already present and attempting to explain to the Director what happened. The Director looked at me and said, "I have no complaints! You are doing a good job! Thank you!"

Months later, after directors had changed, Ray came to me again and said, "Hey, I see you live in Schaumburg and I have a friend who is the manager of the respiratory department at a hospital there. She needs a critical care therapist and I think you would be excellent for the position." This was a tempting offer since it was close to where I lived. I knew he was trying to get rid of me, but taking this job would give me another three hours a day to be home because it would eliminate travel time spent on the expressway. I applied for the position and was called in for an interview. Overall, the interview went well but the manager did not think that I would be a good fit because I was 55 years old. I left the interview thinking her loss!!! A few days later, I received a phone call from the hospital near my home offering me the job! I accepted the offer! I was eligible for retirement from my current hospital so I retired on Friday and began my new job the following Monday!

The new job was perfect! I now had the most wonderful boss in the world and I worked with the most wonderful people in the world. I loved them and I felt their love for me every day especially when they began calling me "Mama Sheila." The work of respiratory therapy is very hard mentally, emotionally and physically. I would never have been able to work until age 71 without their support. Throughout my career the Lord worked miracles in my life and the life of my patients.

Choose Christ
By: Denise Hartung – Manuel

And if it seem evil unto you to serve the LORD, choose you this day whom ye will serve; (Joshua 24:15a)

"I hear the Lord saying, 'Choose Christ,'" Apostle Henderson said. It was the night I had first met Prophet Tiffany and Apostle Larry Henderson. I was standing in their living room, I was in bondage, and they were attempting to deliver me. At the time, I believed my bondage was to drugs, crack to be specific. I had been struggling to get clean for months after having relapsed. I prayed, and I read my Bible, I listened to every Christian message I could get my hands on. I read every book on deliverance, on knowing God, on finding my purpose. I did absolutely everything I could think of, but I could NOT get clean. I did not understand why I was stuck in this nightmare again, as I watched testimony after testimony of people who had been miraculously delivered, I felt like I was missing some important ingredient to this faith thing. I was desperate to have whatever was missing, I felt like I would surely do anything to be free. I went to see Prophet and Apostle that night to find the answers I desperately needed, to find my miraculous deliverance. In some ways I did, but it was not at all what I had expected.

I originally got clean because I had gone to prison. I had been living a life far from God for a very long time. I had made poor choice after poor choice for most of my life.

Always chasing after the love I had not found in my childhood, the acceptance I had never known. I made myself a promise when I was just a little girl, you see. I promised myself that one day I was going to be loved, and I was going to have the family I didn't have growing up. Yes, one day someone was going to love me and make me feel special and safe - no matter what! I must have been around 5 or 6 years old when I made that inner vow, when I built that stronghold to protect myself from the pain of rejection. The enemy went to work right away, turning what I had built to protect myself, into a stronghold which would keep me bound in countless ways, making me a slave to those emotions. You see, the enemy helped to fortify the stronghold I had set up myself. Over the years he had whispered many lies in my ear, and he reinforced every painful rejection, he used every choice to draw me further into darkness. I never had a chance really, I had no idea I even had an enemy, let alone that I was helping him to destroy me.

I have come to understand, choosing Christ is not a one and done endeavor. I am faced with many situations in which I will either choose Christ, or not, every day. I am also faced with pivotal moments in my relationship with my Father, in which He asks me once again to define the relationship. He wants to know, am I committed? Do I trust Him? Will I obey? Or will we have to wrestle again?

I believed that I had already chosen Christ, so I was confused by what was being said. When I asked, "What does that mean? Choose Christ." The only response I got was a repeat of what had already been said. Huh, wasn't that just like God, always with some cryptic answer?

In my experience, the Lord often leads with a hint, a mystery of sorts. Rarely have I gotten a direct instruction or specific Word right from the start. As frustrating as that has been, I recognize the Lord has done this out of His Love for me. He has been extremely gentle, always patient, and incredibly kind to me. The truth is, I was quite wounded when He began courting me, battered would be a better description, and I was in no way prepared to see what He has since revealed to me. That is why I say He was and still is a God of hints and clues at first, He reveals truth to me, about me, but he often does it in small increments, over time, until the time is exactly right for me to be able to handle that truth. Like I said, I was battered, too fragile to see the truths he had for me in the light of His love, I would have been crushed under the weight of some of those truths, if not for the gentleness of my Father. I would later discover that wasn't the entire picture. In fact, I was in bondage to many things.

I finally decided to try what the Henderson's had been saying and "Choose Christ!" I realized that I had chosen my boyfriend over God every time. I would rather be with him and receive his love (and drugs) rather than receive the fullness of Christ. I chose to move out of our apartment together as a first step to maintain my sobriety. I then enrolled myself in community college and made a choice to choose God every day. Every day I chose to catch the bus, go to school, go to work and sever the relationships upon which I had become dependent. The more I chose God, the longer I maintained my sobriety. By the time I celebrated 3 years of sobriety I also graduated from community college and enrolled in a university!

I have now graduated with a Bachelor's degree in Social Work, I'm working on my Master's degree and I am a certified Drug and Alcohol Misuse Counselor that is still sober and choosing Christ every day!

In The Fight For My Life
By: Roselyn Forbes

For I am persuaded, that neither death, nor life, nor angels, nor principalities, nor powers, nor things present, nor things to come, nor height, nor depth, nor any other creature, shall be able to separate us from the love of God, which is in Christ Jesus our Lord. (Romans 8:38, 39)

"Why do you drink those?" he said referring to my Amaretto Stone Sour. "Because they taste good," I snarled back. I looked down at my buzzing phone. It was my sister Monique. Why is she calling me so late I thought? I answered the phone, "Hey Mo, what's up?" "Ma told me to come get you," she said, "Keith is in the hospital. Are you at your dorm?" "No, I just got off work," I answered, "I'm at Miller's Pub on Wabash." "Ok, head back to your dorm. I'm on my way now to come get you," she said. "But why, I have so much work to do tomorrow before classes on Monday," I asked. "Just head back to your dorm. I don't know. Ma wouldn't tell me what happened. She said I had to come get you and she'd tell us when we got to the hospital," she urged. "Ok, fine. I'll meet you in front of my dorm," I replied.

As I paid my tab and gathered my things to leave, anger started to well up in me. I began to think, what did he do now? Why do I have to leave school because Keith did something stupid and sprang his leg or arm or whatever? I have so much stuff to do!

As I walked back toward the dorms, my thoughts became angrier and more upset that this was disrupting my plans. I began to think about all I had left to do. I have to finish my theory homework and rehearse for vocalese. Oh man, I still have to finish that diction assignment. Ugh, I better bring some of my work. At least I can work on stuff in the waiting room. I finally get into Roosevelt and find a place I feel I belong and now I have to be pulled back home to be there for Keith's drama. And Ma, she knows how important this is to me why is she doing this? My thoughts began to spin out of control and I became more and more filled with frustration and anger.

The whole ride out to the hospital all I could think was how much stuff I had to do and wonder how long I'd have to stay there. We arrived at the hospital and parked. When we walked up we saw my ma and dad standing outside with *some* of the rest of the family. As we got closer, my dad yells out, "Keith's gone!" We said, "What do you mean he's gone? Where did he go? Where did they take him?" "Keith is dead," he said. I was confused thinking he was playing some cruel joke because I could tell he had been drinking. "Keith's dead," he said again, "he died."

I looked at my sister, Roshaunda and my brother in-law Mark. Roshaunda looked like she had been crying. "What happened," I asked. "A nun hit him," I heard, not registering who said it. The next hour or so was a blur as we waited to see him.

They escorted us into a room where he was lying on a table. His body was still a little warm, but lifeless. Not at all like the animated and loveable little brother I had known. It still hadn't set in for me that he was dead. Even seeing him lying there on the table it didn't feel real. It felt like I was walking through a scene from a movie or TV show as one of the characters.

I don't remember crying much in the days after. When I wasn't planning and coordinating his funeral, I was out drinking and not being alone. I spent nights with my ex-boyfriend and nights with my best friend's ex-boyfriend. Even though she said it was ok I knew it was wrong, but at that time I didn't care who I was hurting. I was so broken that nothing mattered anymore. My little brother was taken out by someone who had vowed to spend the rest of her life to serve God and by serving people. Why should I care if this could happen and in this way? How could He let this happen? How could it have been his servant that killed my little brother?

I ended up coordinating a lot for the services and helping my parents with different things. My family all had children to help through this tragedy or were understandably, barely functional at the time. For some reason, I stuffed mine down and it hit me later in unexpected ways at random times. When I tried to return to school, I would see Keith standing in my classrooms or see him turning the corner in a hall and break down. The only thing I *could* do was go to work. Work helped to keep my head clear and distracted. When I wasn't at work I used *other distractions* to keep the thoughts at bay. Being alone at night was unbearable because of all the thoughts that would flood my mind, so I made sure that I wasn't alone often. At school, there were weeks of randomly crying uncontrollably in class *and all over the school.* This was exacerbated by no longer having any drive to complete course work or even go to class at times, so I decided to take a medical leave from school. My sister and brother in-law took me in and let me stay with them. When I moved in with them, I left my job in the city as well because the commute would be too much. I was out of work for about three months. I just coasted, going out with whoever was willing till all hours of the night. Suffice it to say, my sister and brother in-law were very understanding.

God? Humph, I was so angry at him. There were times I felt like I hated him. Like everything I learned in church growing up about how much he loved me was a lie; like he lied to me.

Some days I thought I was fine. Some I was just numb, but other days I didn't know what to do with myself. Most of the time I hated myself. I hated myself for being angry at Keith when he died. I hated myself for not taking the time when I had it to spend time with him. I always thought I'd have the time to be close to him when we got older. Keith was always just my annoying little brother, drumming on whatever was near and constantly asking for stuff. I figured we'd have a better relationship later on. I thought I had the time.

After Keith died, something died in me. I no longer cared about anything. I didn't care about what I was doing or what the consequences were; I didn't even think about them. I did what felt good in the moment. I carried on like this for a long time after he died. I got serving job after serving job and I kept coasting thinking I was moving on. One night following a random crying fit, I was on Facebook and I commented on a post from an old friend from my childhood church, Reggie. Something in his post spoke to me in my rut. He invited me to come to a Bible study. It wasn't at the church so I felt like maybe it would be ok. I hadn't been able to step foot back in the church since Keith's funeral. It was just too hard. There were too many memories of the three of us (me, our sister Azzie and Keith) growing up there. We spent so much time there in programs and ministries. It was like a second home.

I went to the Bible study and it was unlike any Bible study I had ever attended. It was intense. I mean they studied the Greek *and* Hebrew words as well as the definitions behind them. They showed me how to go into the word and how to let it interpret itself, so I could understand it. They were speaking in tongues which I had heard of, but never seen or heard first hand. I thought it was only for the church elders or really *holy* people. Either way, it was really different, intimidating and a bit scary to be honest. I think Reggie could tell I was scared because he came up to me after and said, "I know it is different, but you should come back." It felt way over my head, but it had been almost three years of coasting. I was yearning for something different and this, this was definitely different.

I came back and it wasn't so much of a culture shock. This time I had a chance to take in what was being taught because it wasn't so bracing. I became intrigued and then enthralled. It was like opening a door to a whole new world that was always there in front of me, but I couldn't see it; like I wasn't wearing the right set of glasses. I found a whole new way of looking at something that I had seen all my life. The Bible wasn't a fairytale book anymore, it was a tangible guide on how to operate this Christian walk. This was the life line I needed. This had the power to snap me out of my haze and give me something to hold on to. It felt like seeing the glimmer of light at the end of a very long and dark tunnel. Suddenly, the Bible was a love letter from my Creator to me. It felt like he was talking directly to me; like he was reaching out to me. He told me that he felt my hurt, my pain. He said that he saw me the whole time and I realized that he had been watching over me. He had been keeping me safe from the drinking and driving, from the sex I was having that could've resulted in pregnancy or disease, from the depression that made me want to drive over the highway divider into the next lane or right over the overpass, nose diving into the traffic below and from the feeling of being lonely and unlovable. For so many reasons, I felt like I was an awful person who had done awful, awful things. I still to this day call it my dark year because there was such a darkness that entered my life in that time from Keith's death and all the things I was doing to avoid dealing with it.

After many counseling sessions and even some deliverance, I started to feel okay again. I began to heal. I started to work multiple jobs which kept me busy, but also kept me from going back to the Kingdom Advancement Center's (KAC) Bible Study. More time passed and eventually, I started to date someone. We were bopping around to a few different churches. I took him to the KAC and he wasn't a fan. The one thing I remember is Prophet Henderson coming up to us to make it known to him that they had my back and they loved me. Now, I hadn't been there for a few years at this point, but they still thought of me as family. This touched me more than they will ever know and it was then that I knew I needed to come back. I began to come on my own and I would feel so free during worship like I felt when I was a kid. One Sunday, I felt tears stream down my face and I didn't know why. I was feeling happy so why was I crying? It was joy unspeakable, immeasurable joy. I felt a connection that I hadn't felt before. I had a warmth and comfort that I can't even explain. That Sunday in praise and worship I told Jesus Christ that I couldn't do it on my own anymore and I welcomed Him back into my life.

It is crazy how fast God begins to work in your life when you let him in. I was baptized again on June 7, 2015. I had been baptized when I was a kid, but there is something different about making the decision as an adult to follow Him. In the fall of 2015, my boyfriend and I parted ways. God had been trying to show me that he wasn't who he had for me, but I would make excuses for keeping him in my life. That was a hard time, but He needed to break off what wasn't good for me to make room for all the blessings he had in store for me. I had gotten a full-time job and by that same fall, I no longer needed to have my two other part time jobs, bartending and running photo booths for events. By February of 2016, I was already back in school working on my bachelor's degree and He wasn't done there. Later, I found out that this full-time job was a stepping stone because in April of 2016 I got another full-time job earning almost double what I was making before. At some point, I joined the KAC praise team and he continued to break things off me through my praise and worship time with him. There were Sundays that I would cry and sing through the tears as I could feel emotional weight melt off me.

My life continued to flourish and even though I had dealt with Keith's death, all along there was something that continued to gnaw at me. I was learning all about the gifts and about the power God has given us. The guilt of not knowing Keith more before he died and knowing where he was spiritually when he died ate at me. Knowing that we have the power to raise people from the dead and the thought that if I had known then what I know now, maybe he would still be here. My sister, Azzie, had told me that he was a believer and that he was saved, but for some reason I couldn't put it down. I received a breakthrough in May of 2018 when the women of the church decided to go on a Women's Retreat. We shared and learned things about each other. During one of our sessions, I was sharing my story of Keith's death and about the guilt I felt with not knowing for sure if he was saved. When I was done, Korei Mullins, our facilitator, stood up and reassured me that she knew for sure that he was saved. She explained how she taught him in her Sunday school class and how he knew the Word and he knew Jesus Christ as his Savior. She told me there was no doubt that he was saved. At that moment, the last part of the guilt and upset I had concerning his death broke off me. I was finally free! It had been 11 years since his death and a long process, but God made sure that I was in the right place at the right time to be able to receive my full healing.

Where am I now? I am loving and growing in my role as a worship leader. I continue to grow in Christ every day. I have completed my degree and I am realizing that He truly wants so much more for me in my life than I ever imagined. His plan for me is so much larger than what I had planned for my life. I am looking forward to owning multiple businesses and in the process of dreaming up and discovering what my future may look like with Jesus Christ at the helm guiding me. I thank Him every day for rescuing me and I am constantly in awe of what he has done for, in and through me.

Living Life on Purpose
Questions for Reflection/Discussion

1. Define the word purpose. What does it mean to you? How do you know when you have found it?

2. Think about your current career path. How did you get into this field? Is your current career connected to your purpose? Why? Why not?

3. Find biblical examples of someone (other than Jesus) living out their purpose. What is the difference between how the biblical character came to understand their purpose and how you are or are not understanding your purpose?

4. Reflect on situations where you thought it would end one way but the Lord had other plans better than your desired outcome. What was your behavior, thoughts or actions while God's superior plan was unfolding? What did you learn about yourself in the process? What did you learn about God?

5. Choose an author from this Section of the book whose story resonates with you. Why is their story meaningful to you? How would you handle the situation if you were in their shoes?

6. Write down what you believe is God's purpose for your life. Why is this your purpose? What scriptures do you have to support this view?

7. If you know your purpose, are unsure about your purpose or do not have a clue about your purpose, pray about your purpose! Ask God to give you more revelation and insight into His plan for your life according James 1: 5, 6.

We Don't Look Like What We've Been Through

PART III
WE ARE PRECIOUS IN HIS SIGHT

Then said Saul, I have sinned: return, my son David: for I will no more do thee harm, because my soul was precious in thine eyes this day: behold, I have played the fool, and have erred exceedingly. (1 Samuel 26:21)

In First Samuel, we learn about the tumultuous relationship between Saul the ousted King and David the anointed King. Saul was chosen by the people, but rejected by God. Through the spirit of rejection he projected his anger from losing his position and power toward David who served him faithfully. Saul sought to kill David even though David never committed any evil act toward his king. In the scripture above, we find Saul repenting for trying to kill David because David proved he had opportunity to kill Saul but did not take it. David pled with Saul to stop his unwarranted pursuit and allow him to live. In Saul's surrendering soliloquy, he confesses his sin to David in full realization that his "soul was precious" to his perceived enemy. Even though David had every right and opportunity to kill the person making every effort to murder him, he chose not to do so. David still saw value and worth in Saul despite the actions of the wicked king. *And David said to Abishai, Destroy him not: for who can stretch forth his hand against the Lord's anointed, and be guiltless?* (1 Samuel 26:9) David recognized that even though Saul was wicked, he was still the Lord's anointed. Saul's soul was still precious, meaning of great value and not to be treated carelessly.

This is how the Lord sees us, His people. We behave wickedly, and go out of our way to carry out our own personal agendas with no regard for him who loves us. In spite of our actions, worthy of death at times, the Lord chooses to let us live. He still has precious thoughts toward us. *How precious also are thy thoughts unto me, O God! How great is the sum of them!* (Psalm 139:17) He continues to assign value and worth to us as His precious creation even when we, like Saul, play the fool and have erred exceedingly.

The women in Part III reveal through the deliverance of great trials and tribulations, that we are indeed precious (of great value) to the Lord. The authors tell of how God pulled them out of abusive relationships, healed them of physical illnesses, delivered them from addiction and lust and provided peace in the midst of chaos and confusion. The power of God to love and keep them even when they didn't acknowledge him, shows just how precious we are to Him. The Lord has precious thoughts toward us and he only wants the best for us all!

STILL STANDING!
By: ANONYMOUS

Be not afraid of the king of Babylon, of whom ye are afraid; be not afraid of him, saith the LORD: for I am with you to save you, and to deliver you from his hand. (Jeremiah 42:11)

My childhood memories are riddled with abuse. My mother would beat me and speak vile words toward me projecting her thoughts that I would never amount to anything, and that I wasn't going to make it in life! I grew up feeling like I would never be enough in my mother's eyes, yet I loved her still. I grew up without my natural Father who at some point denied I belonged to him because he already had a family. Even though these are the two individuals you would think a child should have a close relationship with, I was very distant and unconnected from both my parents and felt alone in the world. I didn't realize how much I needed an earthly Father to tell me he loved me, or how proud he was of me until, I had children of my own and realized the importance of a Father's role. The only person in my life to fill that role was my mother, who would instead, abuse me emotionally and physically. As an adult, I now realize the void in my life from the lack of a healthy relationship with my parents, was the primary reason I almost lost my life from the abuse by my high school boyfriend.

At the age of 14, I entered into my first serious relationship with a guy to whom I gave my whole heart. He was everything to me. He was my breath of fresh air, my soul, and a part of me. I gave this person my whole heart and all of me. We dated throughout high school and early college years and I knew one day I would be his wife! Everyone would comment on how cute we were and how close we were to each other. I wanted to see him every day, I thought of him all day and I was always excited to be around him. However, my life drastically changed the first time he pushed me down really hard and pretended it was an accident. These "accidents" became more and more frequent as I would begin taking blows to the face with black eyes, getting kicked, and strangled. This relationship I was so excited about changed into a very dangerous situation for any woman to endure and I didn't know what to do. I could not talk to my mom and her boyfriend about this terrible situation as I didn't have a healthy relationship with them either. I continued to press through daily even though the situation grew worse and worse. One evening, I was at work as a waitress late at night and no one was in the restaurant except a Police Officer who was sitting in the corner. I walked past the Officer heading to one of my tables that needed to be cleaned and he said really softly, "He is going to kill you if you don't leave." I said, "Excuse me?" He said it again, "He is going to kill you if you don't leave." The Officer continued to say, "I see he fractured your eye!" That night I felt that God was trying to tell me something! I began to think about all of the beatings, emotional abuse and the time he put a gun to my head. I thought no matter what it takes, it's time to leave now! I knew it was not going to end well but if I stayed, it could be death for me. I went to my apartment and broke off the relationship. He beat me up so bad I wound up in the hospital. Even though I was in the hospital I was happy because I felt free! While I was in the hospital he stole my car and put it into a ditch and I didn't even care because I was free now with no more abuse in my life.

One year later, I came home to get ready for my college football game only to realize my ex-boyfriend found my new apartment, broke in and hid in the closet. He forced himself on me sexually, then left. I hear people talk about what they would do if something like this happened to them, but you have no idea how you would process such a tragic event until you're in it. Broken, disgusted and feeling somewhat at fault for what just happened to me, I pulled myself together and got dressed. When I got to the game, I told some of my friends what happened so they followed me home. When we arrived we noticed that all of my lights were on and they figured he had returned. They were right. That night did not end too well for him. My friends beat him up pretty bad and he left for good, never to return again. I continued my life feeling free.

Weeks later, I felt strange in my body, so I went to the doctor and found out I was pregnant. I sat in that office shocked, devastated and unable to move for a while. I couldn't believe I was pregnant by the person who beat and raped me. My life was forever changed, again. Many of my friends and family told me it was not a good idea to keep this child considering what happened to me. I decided to keep my child as it was not the child's fault how their conception occurred. I knew I would love this child and that we would be ok. I gave birth and took care of my baby and moved on with life putting my trust in the Lord!

Even with all of the trying times I faced dealing with abuse, the Lord still covered me. I am a true believer that the Lord knows the plans that he has for all of us! Even though not knowing my earthly Father and not having a close relationship with my Mother may have opened an insecurity in me to be in such a terrible relationship with someone who hurt me so badly, God is still Faithful! I'm Still Standing! During those times, I wasn't saved and the Lord still protected me. I gave my life to the Lord and have never looked back. I'm not angry, hurt or holding on to unforgiveness. I am free and experiencing life more abundantly in Jesus Name!

From My Back to My Knees!
By: Kellie Murphy

I say unto you, that likewise joy shall be in heaven over one sinner that repenteth, more than over ninety and nine just persons, which need no repentance. (Luke 15:7)

It's amazing how I've never really paid attention to the baseboards being so far off the ground. You can't help but notice when lying face down on the carpet staring at the base boards. I thought to myself maybe when I finally get up I can actually inquire about them. The spasm in my back has finally gone away and now would be a good time to attempt to use my arms to push myself up. Finally, I am up and can crawl my way over to the couch so I can properly sit down and reflect on how I ended up in this situation.

Thinking back over the last few months, things have been extremely stressful. I kept up my responsibilities at church, working late hours at my job and driving almost an hour away from my apartment. The extra stress has shown up in my shoulders and back. I just have not been able to settle myself down. I am feeling the pressures of my responsibilities. Church was usually a place of peace after a crazy work day, but lately, the cares of supporting multiple ministries, feeling underappreciated in the process and the lack of suitable dating prospects have stolen my joy, now, serving is more of a chore than a blessing.

My job on the other hand, is high intensity where I listen to customers whine and complain all day long about something as minor as a cell phone bill! Sure, they have become popular to where more people have a cell phone than a landline phone, but still, it is not as serious as some customers are making out. However, I really do not plan to stay on my job very long. I only want to save up enough money to pay off my student loans and move on to become a counselor.

Moving this far away from where I work was not a part of the plan either; however, the rent in the area I'd like to live compared to my current budget doesn't exactly see eye to eye. Plus, I just left a roommate situation, so it is time to enjoy the benefits of affording my rent and living on my own. I should be enjoying this time in my life, but my body hasn't gotten the message.

Can you move your feet?

The first thing I received after arriving to Sherman Hospital that evening was a full body MRI scan. The results uncovered two benign masses intertwined within my spinal cord. One mass the size of a quarter was on the left side and a second mass was found on the right side of my spine. At last, the mystery was solved; I had a Schwannoma tumor! Now it is time to get this thing out of me without any paralysis.

My surgeon introduced himself to me and my family and offered words of encouragement to my family, as he explained his approach to remove the tumor in order to alleviate the pain in my body. The one thing he mentioned prior to the surgery was, you will know if it was successful if you can wiggle your toes afterwards. That night I had time to reflect on all the events leading up to this moment right before my surgery. I was thankful that the tumor was discovered and it was not cancer and there is a working plan to remove it. I am thankful for my faith to believe nothing less than total body recovery and no paralysis. I am also thankful for the HMO insurance coverage, because even though things were mixed up and confused, this surgery will be covered. With so many things to be thankful for, I still feel like something is missing. I could have died before reaching the age of 30 and what do I really have to show for myself? I am not married, nor do I have any children, sure I have a college degree, but am I using it or working to my full capacity? There has got to be more to my life than just going to work, church and the occasional movie. After I make a full recovery, I will make a total lifestyle change. God would not want me to live an incomplete life.

I went off to surgery and the first thing my mother did after the surgery was throw the covers off my legs and shout: "Kellie, wiggle your toes!" they wiggled. I could barely open my eyes, nor was I completely sure what she was saying, but I remembered the doctors words and I moved my feet. A feeling of joy and excitement came over both of us and there, in that moment, we knew the surgery had been a success and I'd be alright. Now the recovery work begins.

The physical therapy process was rough, but having my life back was worth the fight. I have new bucket list items like: driving a sports car, getting married and carrying a child, which I had to ensure my body would hold up to the task.

At last year 30 had arrived. No, this is not exactly what I planned for my life but I promised myself I would start truly living from this point forward. My friends would be new.

The old ones are welcome to come along with me on my new journey, but not all may approve and I cannot have their guilt on my hands. I can move out of my mother's house and into my own place in the city. As grateful as I was to stay with my mother while I recovered, it is truly time for me to live on my own. I will finally meet men, which is most important to me. My dating life has been non-existent up until this point, but I am eager to get out there and take my chances. I mean, they can't be any worse than what I've witnessed inside of the church, right?

It was with these words I walked bright eyed and falsely equipped into my 30's. I believed I was drawn to live a "richer" life and that life was not going to be found sitting in church, but instead I had to go out and experience what life had to offer me.

In the beginning, I had FUN! Finally, the way I wanted to live life was up to ME. Sure, the voice of the Lord was still present in my ear, but I told myself I wouldn't go too far off the deep end because I was grown and knew better. My new outlook on life brought me new friends and we danced, partied and celebrated life in what we thought was harmless fun. The more we paraded around the city looking for excitement, the greater the thrill of being noticed. The voice of the Lord was present in my ear but, the thrill of being noticed spoke louder.

For the first time in my adult life, I not only felt sexy, but I carried myself in such a way that men were drawn to me and I was addicted to it. I was confident, bold, self-assured, and ready to receive whoever came my way. I took pride in honing the art of seduction to see who I could draw and how long it took for them to succumb to me. The city was my playground and my body was compelled to explore this new found sexual freedom. But what I did not factor, I almost lost my soul in the process of living my experiences. The Lord healed my back and I began to use it for the pleasure of men and not the will of God. The voice of the Lord was still present, ever so faintly and far less frequent than before.

By the time I reached 38, I was ready for the life experience to end. The art of seduction lead me into a war zone of tormented loneliness. Each encounter became increasingly less about pleasure, but more of an enslavement to obey the lustful act. I wanted the experience to end, but I no longer believed I could simply just stop. I had drifted so far away from the life I imagined in my hospital recovery bed and I found myself slipping into a state of loneliness and depression. Where was the voice of the Lord? I can't seem to hear it. It was there before, how can I find it? There is no place I can run to quiet the loneliness in my heart. I am in desperate need to hear God's voice again.

My thoughts drifted back to an earlier time of desperation for God, so I prayed. I remembered how he heard my heart's cry. This time, I got off my back and knelt down on my knees! But now, only my arms are opened wide to completely surrender and receive the full love and forgiveness of God. In my compulsion, a child was conceived so my prayers were not just for me but for the child inside of me. My cry was heard and my prayers answered. The Lord gave me grace through the gift of my son and he is a living reminder not to return to my old way of living.

I now hear my Father's voice louder than any strange compulsion. The Lord answered my prayers by gracefully breaking me down out of that self - centered, destructive lifestyle for good. My new purpose was found in believing I am loved, accepted and I belong in the Kingdom of God. Instead of chasing after fools, I can be found in the embrace of my Father's arms.

Have You Considered...
By: Minister Nikki Palmer

For we wrestle not against flesh and blood, but against principalities, against powers, against the rulers of the darkness of this world, against spiritual wickedness in high places. (Ephesians 6:12)

I woke that morning with a knot in my stomach from anxiety. Not that, "Christmas morning heading to the tree anxiety," but the kind that causes your breathing to be labored, your thoughts to be scattered and your emotions to go numb. I planned this day with the same detail and oversight I used just five months earlier. However today, the atmosphere wasn't full of laugher, love and possibilities, instead it reeked of death.

Opening the door brought internal conflict. This was the same door that was supposed to house a new beginning. Walking through "this" door was supposed to stir up joy, excitement, occasional disagreements, raw fights, passionate making up and adventure. It was supposed to welcome family, new friends and new life. Inside these walls, God's presence was supposed to be welcomed and the Glory of God was supposed to rest. Instead, this 1300 square foot apartment housed an evil I wasn't prepared to fight. It was here where I began to fear the setting of the sun because bad things happened in the dark. It took a little over a week to secure a moving van and helping hands to help move. That morning I waited until I could confirm he was at work and then without hesitation, the same people who were part of my wedding party became my moving crew. We moved quickly and without much conversation. While my friends and family placed books and dishes in boxes I felt like I was in a bad movie, somewhere in between, "Enough" with Jennifer Lopez and Tyler Perry's, "The Diary of a Mad Black Woman" and I couldn't wake up. As I moved from room to room I wanted to breakdown. I wanted to literally lay down and give in to the pain that consumed my mind and heart. I logically understood I had to go, that he wanted me to go. I still had the text message from him that read: "I don't want you in my bed and I don't want to be married to you anymore," that's clear, right? My mind understood, but there was still part of me that hoped he would come through the door and promise once again to have and to hold me in sickness and in health, for better or for worse, to cherish and love me. See, that's the deception mental abuse creates. It causes the lines between good and evil, logical and illogical, safe and unsafe to be blurred. It paints the illusion that the same man who a month earlier forcefully took from his wife what I had willingly vowed to freely give and when he finished only replied "a husband can't rape his wife," could love me respectfully and completely. My marriage was never a marriage and my husband was never a husband, logically I knew that, but emotionally I struggled with the "why."

    The abuse didn't start off blatantly, though it started immediately after our wedding day. Within weeks, of standing before God, family and friends and exchanging vows, the man that promised to be my protector became my abuser. He started by forbidding me to touch his cell phone, saying that if I needed or even wanted to know who he communicated with, I was a weak woman. Two weeks to the date of our wedding, he sat me down to tell me that the financial planning we had agreed to practice would not happen. He coldly explained that I would be lucky if he paid the rent and from that day forward, his money was just that, his. Three weeks in, while at a family BBQ he parked the car alone at Montrose Beach and later told me to find it among thousands of beach goers. The first week he didn't come home until near morning two days in a row and I asked him about it, he drew me close into his arms, looked gently into my eyes and whispered, "None of your damn business." Then there were the days he would call me at work sounding like the other him, those days he would come home with fresh flowers and an emotional apology. We would go to dinner and he would promise to be different, he'd promise to be who I thought he was, that only lasted a day or so.

    There were several days he would request a special meal. I would shop, prep and prepare everything to his liking, only to get a phone call hours later saying, he didn't want my cooking and he was eating out. When he did come home after work, the nights were filled with him telling me everything I wasn't. He seemed to take great joy in speaking hateful words. He would say, that I couldn't do anything right, that I was clingy and needy and I was weak. He often reminded me that black women have the highest rate of being unmarried and because of that if I wanted to be married to a black man, I would have to deal with something. His closing signature statement was that no one else wanted me and that was why I was single for so long. I would try not to break down in front of him, but I couldn't contain the pain, the fear, hurt and the disappointment which flooded my face with every tear. Even though I received that text message, I didn't leave then. No, I stayed and woke early every morning and made him breakfast, made sure his work uniform was clean and ready and then I would pray. I would pray that if I was strong enough and showed him the love of God through my actions that he would come to his senses. But instead his actions and treatment towards me worsened. He did confirm that he had not been and had never planned to be monogamous. The same night he declared he had a real woman, he got dressed put on some good smelling cologne and laughed at me on his way out. His relationship with another woman would be confirmed and once it was, he did nothing to hide it.

I thought the first emotion I would feel was anger but instead the first emotion I encountered was shame. See, I was known by family and friends as a bold, outspoken, energetic, talkative, active, people loving extrovert. I would tell it like it was with no invitation and make friends standing in the DMV line in a heartbeat. Now, I was meek and not in a good way. I found myself begging for the man who willingly vowed his love for me to spend an hour at home. For the first time in my Christian life, I felt alone.

He would sometimes say he was waiting for me to drop the good church girl act. The very thing he said he loved about me, he now seemed to resent. I loved Jesus! I was active at my church for a decade and had served in children's ministry 15 years by the time I met him. I loved Jesus and I loved serving Jesus. I would talk to anyone who would listen and some who wouldn't about the amazing grace and powerful love of Jesus. This was what I was doing when I met him. During our season of dating, we would spend hours talking about the Bible and our personal relationships with God as well as our church involvement and history. When marriage was put on the table, we both communicated the desire to remain sexually pure and not live together or have sex until we were married. He called every morning Monday through Friday at 6 am to pray with me the entire time we dated and were engaged. I began attending the church he attended where he was part of the men's ministry and several of his (married) family members attended. He used to give me cards weekly during our dating season and when he smiled, I saw years of tomorrows in his eyes. I was in love. In love with a man that loved God. A man that was pursuing the heart of God. He wasn't perfect and nor was I, but together we were going to advance the Kingdom of God. When he said he loved me, I believed him and when he said I was an answer to his prayers I believed that he was also the answer to mine. I must admit he didn't have the same level of understanding as I did about the bible. For years as a single woman I was accused of having standards too high for any man to reach. People in and out of the church would say, "Nikki is waiting to marry Jesus." His desire and commitment to learn silenced my concerns. But now, I couldn't help but think was this a red flag?

Within four months of being married my physical appearance had drastically changed, much like the man I married. I weighed less than 100 pounds, my eyes were a deep red all the time and I was experiencing hair loss. For the first time in my Christian walk I felt forsaken. How could my Lord, my Father allow this to happen to me? As a 22-year-old woman I gave my whole life to Jesus and now I felt like I was being rejected by God.

One morning, I woke up to breakfast fixed for me and an invitation to spend time together that evening. It was that night, under the dim lights of one of my favorite restaurants that he explained that our marriage could work, that there was something "I could" indeed do to save our marriage. He explained that I read the bible and went to church too much. He went on to say that was good for when we were dating and engaged but we didn't need church now. Gently reaching over he cupped my hand and said, I needed to put the bible down and start listening to only him. This can't be real, I thought. He can't seriously be asking me to do that. When I didn't agree and reminded him I was reading my bible, serving and going to church when he met me, after we began dating, while we were engaged and that we did the same together, he told me if I wasn't willing to change then I had to go. He said he was filing for divorce. He had no desire to get counseling or to work things out. He also said he would not stop his other relationship. When I came home from work the next day he had divorce papers waiting for me on the bed in the guest room.

My first night officially gone, I called my sisters and cried, I kept asking why? Why me? My middle sister calmly said, "Nikki, why not you?" She asked me to go reread the book of Job. As I read through the book of Job I began asking the question. Did what I fear come upon me? I asked God to show me what I couldn't see. Then these words jumped out at me, HAVE YOU CONSIDERED MY SERVANT JOB? (Job 1:8.) I wasn't saying of myself that I was perfect like the Lord said of Job, that wasn't it. I had spent so much time trying to figure out what I had done wrong that I never thought that this trial, this test, this tribulation came because of what I was doing right. I had long given up the thought that my Christian life would be one of smooth sailing, that hardship would pass me by like death passed by the children of Israel. What was right was my commitment to Jesus. Up until then, I thought I had experienced loss and even pain. I walked away from fires, cancer scares, financial hardships and friends that left. I walked away from these circumstances, but the death of my marriage was something I would have to walk through. As I read the book of Job I could hear God say, "Will you worship me still? When it looks, feels and sounds like I've gone silent will you still trust me?" My answer was yes. That day, I told God that no matter the situation, I would trust him. I prayed that my marriage could be restored but I would not forsake God in the process.

I spent several weeks in counseling with a professional (yes, I saw a shrink) and I entered in to a time of fasting and prayer. I wasn't interested in the right or wrongs or pointing fingers, I was seeking the truth. Although I was uncertain about so much at that point in my life there was one thing I still believed. I still believed that God loved me and that his purpose for my life would be fulfilled. I still believed that God wanted to and would use my life for His glory. I must warn you, God is a God of his Word. If you ask him to show you, You, He will. God revealed A LOT to me about me. I was fearful, a people pleaser and I didn't trust God completely for the true desires of my heart. I allowed years of religious teaching (man's opinion as God's doctrine), other people's opinions and my own insecurities to influence my decisions. God didn't highlight my shortcomings and character flaws to shame me. He showed me the areas of my life that I hadn't completely surrendered because those areas would have hindered me from living my life completely for Him and in Him. Now that the eyes of my heart had been enlightened and my ears had been cleaned from religion, I was mad and hungry. Mad, that the devil was able to access my life and my marriage, and hungry to know how to close the door on the Adversary. I thought I had safe guarded my life and my marriage and now I saw just how unprotected I was. I was living out a generational curse. This was the evil I wasn't prepared to fight, the things that are unseen. Spiritual warfare is often talked over in churches but not taught.

The truth is, I did miss the signs because I didn't know how to look for them. Ignorance doesn't justify our bad or wrong decisions, it simply reveals which open door our consequences come through. The word of God says, *my people are destroyed for a lack of knowledge.* (Hosea 4:6.) I remember a family member saying that I simply made a bad mistake. I said no, I made a bad decision. I made a decision based on the information I had, the "seen" information. Would things had played out differently with the counsel of an Apostle and Prophet......YES! How do I know? Because it wasn't what I could see that destroyed my marriage and tried to take me out. It was the things I could not see. It wasn't even my now ex-husband, it was principalities, powers, rulers of darkness of this world and wickedness in high places. This was the evil I was unprepared to fight.

I learned there is a difference between going through hell with someone and going through hell because of someone and I learned that I have the power to choose. But more than that, I learned I am responsible for my growth, understanding and application of the Word of God for my life and my calling. Since walking out of divorce court, God has healed many broken places in my mind and heart. I have seen God's grace and tangibly felt His love. I have a new laugh and a new smile.

Though my desire to be a wife and mother have yet to come to pass, my hope is not deferred. I am no longer condemned or ashamed, nor do I fight with regret, instead, I am full. I am grateFUL, thankFUL, prayerFUL, joyFUL and peaceFUL!

Believe Only! When Your Back is Against the Wall
By: Brenda J. Law

But without faith it is impossible to please him: for he that cometh to God must believe that he is, and that he is a rewarder of them that diligently seek him. (Hebrews 11:6)

My faith was the kind of faith that "I believed" as long as I didn't have to prove I believed. Looking back now it was not really faith but hope. I hoped things would turn out alright. I hoped a lot of things until one day hope failed and I had to rely on my faith. What I was afraid of was having my faith tested. A thought not spoken but pondered. I felt like Job when he said, *for the thing which I greatly feared is come upon me* (Job 3:24). This is the situation where your back is against the wall and you have no recourse but your faith. Yea, well, that finally showed up at my door.

It was March 1999 when my daughter and her fiancé came to my office and dropped a bomb shell. She was on spring break from Vanderbilt and her fiancé was on spring break from Tennessee State. Both still in school. "Married?" I shouted surprisingly. "Are you serious?" My blood pressure spiked 10 notches. "I can't afford for you to get married right now," I snorted. "Mom," she said calmly," it's not until next year, March 11th." My blood pressure spiked a couple more notches. "You can't get married that soon," I shouted in my motherly voice. "I need more time." But time was not on my side.

For the next six months I woke up every day thinking about how I could pay for this wedding. Prior to this, the struggle became real after I separated from my husband of 26 years and moved into an apartment. I was barely staying afloat paying my own bills for the first time. My mind was on overload, insomnia set in, and I felt like a walking time bomb. Angry and frustrated I reached out for help. My mom got a credit card in her name and gave it to me. She said whatever you need just put it on the credit card. I was so relieved. Overjoyed, thinking all my troubles were over. I told my daughter the exciting news and what came out of her mouth was devastating. She said "Mom, give it back we're not going to use a credit card." I said "Mama gave it to me. This is her gift to you." She said "No, give it back, God is going to pay for the wedding." I said, "Really Tiff?" I was thinking, now she has really lost it. Does she really believe that? Is her faith that strong? Or do I have any faith at all; this was the most faith defining moment I have ever had thus far in my life. Either I believed her or not. Unfortunately, I struggled with my faith and decided God might need a little help. But the Lord did not need my help. Everything I tried to do fell through and God literally showed me he was in control. Things just started to happen.

While at work one day my daughter came in and told me she found her wedding dress at a boutique downtown. She was so excited because the dress was exactly what she wanted and was on clearance. She ran into my office and said, "Mom!! I found the exact dress I want and it's only $99!" I was happy that she found her dress but inwardly sad that I didn't have the $99 to pay for it. Just as I was trying to figure out a way, my boss came in and said, "$99!" "That's all?" "Are you sure this is the one you want?" "Take my card and go buy that dress!" I just stood there dumbfounded. He continued, "What are you waiting on? Go now and make sure you return my credit card!"

My boss was a very kind, caring, and generous man, so it didn't dawn on me that God could be working through him. Later on, I got a phone call from a friend saying she wanted to buy my daughter's bouquet. I was like wow! Things are really coming together. Over the course of time God allowed the giving to snowball. It was like blessings were falling from the sky. Try to keep up: my daughter had a mysterious surplus on her student account that allowed her to order the invitations, all of the vendors gave us steep discounts on all of the services (catering, florist, DJ, photographer, etc.) my mother paid for the cake (without the credit card), my sisters helped purchase the banquet hall and decorations, my daughters' friends and cousins covered her hair, nails, accessories and spa treatments, the grooms family paid for the photography and their honeymoon and those who didn't know how to help gave monetary gifts in advance. It was unbelievable. By the time March rolled around the weather was cold, snow was predicted and I felt anxiety coming on. I was anxious and nervous and worried. Although many things were paid for, there was still the caterer, whom my sisters had already paid more than half down, the videographer and the DJ. I thought, "Ok I think I can handle this from here. All I need now is to borrow the remaining money that was needed."

The Friday before the wedding, no one would lend me any money. I had very good credit at that time and thought there wouldn't be a problem obtaining a loan from the bank.

I went to two banks and both turned me down. One banker told me, "I'm sorry ma'am. I don't understand why you were not approved. It shows you have good credit." God had been trying to show me all along he was in control. My daughter kept telling me "Mama, God is paying for this wedding." She told me time and time again but I couldn't bring myself to match my faith with her faith. I left the bank in tears, my eyes were drowning in water while crossing lanes on the drive home. The rejection from the bank was the last straw. "God!" I said out loud. While choking and snotty, in broken English, I yelled: "You promised me! You said you would be there for me! You said you would never leave me nor forsake me! Where are you God? Do you hear me? I need you! I need you right now! "I guess God was saving the best for last.

 Upon returning home from the bank, distraught, feeling defeated and helpless, crying confusedly and alone, with no one to turn to, I fell to the floor prostrate before God. Not long after returning home, while still stretched out on the floor in the midst of my sobbing and praying, the phone rang. I'm not even sure why l answered because I didn't have caller I.D. and I didn't want to talk; I was pleading my case to God and didn't want to be disturbed. The lady on the other end of the phone said "Hello, Ms. Law, this is Patricia." I was shocked. Her voice was unfamiliar which is why it was unrecognizable to me. "Hi," I said trembling, voice shaking trying to suck up my tears. She said, "I just called to see how the wedding was going. Is everything ok?" When I stuttered, "N-No," the flood gates opened and I told her everything! She said, "Where do you live?" That's all she asked. I gave her my address and within a half hour, she was knocking at my door. Not knowing what she was going to say or do, thinking she came to console me, she handed me an envelope with over $2,000 dollars in cash. This was the exact amount I needed to pay for everything else!

Needless to say, God showed up and showed out!! God waited until my back was up against the wall and the only way out was through him. It wasn't until I had no other choice but to believe God, that my prayers were answered. Don't wait until your back is against the wall. Believe only… the first time.

My Steps are Ordered by the Lord
By: Tiffin Horton

The steps of a good man are ordered by the LORD: and he delighteth in his way. (Psalm 37:23)

    I had a relatively "normal" childhood. I had the normal growing pains and learning experiences of life. I graduated from high school when I was 17 years old and went to college. After undergraduate school, I went to law school, got married and graduated when I was 24. My husband and I moved to Georgia and I began studying for the bar exam. When I was visited by the Chicken Pox bug that same year, I figured that stress, intense studying, and fatigue were part of my chosen profession and caused my immune system to be compromised. I survived my childhood without getting this disease, but thought it was nothing some calamine lotion wouldn't solve. I thought all I needed was to take vitamins. In my mind, I dismissed the previous two years of "strange symptoms" i.e. driving my stick shift car barefoot due to an inability to feel the bottom of my feet, dizziness while walking, fatigue and sensitivity to heat. However, the first symptom that really caused me concern was failing the Georgia Bar Examination by five points. I reasoned a little more intense studying will ensure success, right? But, adding insult to injury, I failed both the second and third times. I had always performed exceptionally well on any standardized examination. So, this was a fluke, right? My brain had never let me down before, I was so confused. I often asked myself, "Whose body is this?" I made it through Undergrad and Law School just fine and now I can't pass the Bar? After the second and third failures, I was convinced that there was a health problem. My body, from my brain to my feet, was out of sync. I was exhausted all day and hot showers were painful.

I moved back to Illinois near my family, divorced and determined to get answers to move forward with my life. I began praying like never before and started studying for the Bar Exam again. I took the bar in February of 1993 and was diagnosed with Multiple Sclerosis on April 22, 1993. Prior to my diagnosis, I was 27 years old and ready to take on the world. I was a mover and shaker, a person who does not get knocked flat down on her bottom. How could this happen? The loss of my ability to walk and mental "quickness" was devastating. I thought to myself, why did GOD do this to me? Someone like me was not expected to receive a diagnosis greater than a cold.

I had no idea what Multiple Sclerosis was when I received the diagnosis. I thought that I was destined for a wheelchair and would be put in a corner, forgotten and left ALONE. My first thoughts after I was diagnosed were: "My life is over and all of my hopes and dreams are lost forever." As a result of my inability to pass the Bar Exam previously, I would never be able to practice Law. So I thought…

After my diagnosis, I got my bar results back. I passed the bar! Hallelujah! It was after this time that the song <u>Order My Steps</u> by GMWA Women of Worship became my anthem. Months later, I got a great job working for the Department of Children and Family Services. The Lord was ordering my steps! Years later, I was introduced to a great guy from Atlanta through my sister who lived there. She thought we would be a great match. We talked on the phone and eventually met and fell in love. We married in April of 2003, exactly 10 years after my diagnosis when I thought my life would be over! My life was actually flourishing! Not long after we were married the Lord blessed us with a beautiful son, just when I thought I would never be a mother! Now we, as a family follow the Lord as He orders our steps.

Even though the disease continued to debilitate me physically, I still had joy in knowing that the Lord loved me and would heal me. Today, I am a Public Defender, mother of a teenager, wife to a great man and I now have the tingling sensation returning in my feet. The Lord is still ordering my steps and eventually I will be able to physically walk them out!

Finding LIFE in CHRIST through DEATH...of both my Parents
By: Kriste N. Clayton

The thief cometh not, but for to steal, and to kill, and to destroy: I am come that they might have life, and that they might have it more abundantly. (John 10:10)

December 18, 2005 will always be a day I'll never forget. I received multiple calls early in the morning between 6:00am -7:00am. Upon fully waking, I finally answered the second or third call. The news on the other end of the phone was devastating! To my dismay, the caller informed me that my mother had passed away. My mother was gone! The reality that I would never get another day with her, or spend another moment with her was life altering. Forever gone, never hearing her voice again, never seeing her smile, never hearing her say "I Love you!", never hearing her fuss at us and grit her teeth when we were in trouble, never being able to meet and share her love and hugs with my children, never hearing her pray, never being able to get her advice. It was too much for me to bear! There were so many things that I took for granted, thinking that my mother would always be here. She died in her sleep with a smile on her face. I am guessing she saw Jesus and the joy of the Lord was her strength at that very moment. We don't know how long she had been gone, but she was not breathing and cold by the time my sister checked on her early that morning.

I missed my mother's smile immediately, her laughter, and her innate joy. She had the "joy of the Lord" in every minute she was here in her earthly house. There was something about her that was contagious to every person she encountered. I can picture her face, even now, though it has been twelve and a half years since I saw it. If she were here, she would be doting on all her grandchildren, giving them all of her love. What a love! My mom truly embodied and exemplified I John 3:16 ...*we ought to lay down our life for the brethren*. She did that daily, with her love she spread, with the Word of God she spread, with the wisdom of God she spread, all with a smile. I can remember her smile when I accepted Jesus Christ as my Lord and Savior at the age of ten. I vividly remember standing up and walking down the aisle a few feet to the altar to declare before everyone that I wanted to accept Him. Throughout my childhood, I enjoyed reading the Word of God, going to church, Vacation Bible School, memorizing the books of the bible and verses. This was due largely in part to my mother's huge influence on me spiritually. She was a strong Woman of God who walked with the Lord and taught me how to walk with the Lord through her example. She and I went everywhere together. We did everything together. I wanted to be like her. She nurtured and guided me, she covered and protected me, taking up for me at all cost.

Throughout my life, my mother's love shielded me from negative and corrupt influences, worldly voices and temptations when I was not spiritually equipped to handle them or make mature decisions and choices. She was the greatest mom, wife, friend, caretaker, aunt, neighborhood block mom, woman on the move for God! I am so blessed to have been graced to see her walk this walk with the Love of the Lord every step of the way. I was determined to live life and be a woman of God who walks the walk and loves fiercely like the example my mother set before me!

When my mother died, though I was hurting and angry, I had to realize that my Father lost his wife of 30 plus years. I saw my Father's strength press through moments of loneliness, pain, and despair. He missed her so much! More than we could begin to understand or imagine. He'd lost his love partner, his confidant, his helpmate, and his mighty Proverbs 31 woman. In the days, months, and years following her death, I could tell that he was heartbroken, but he wouldn't dare let that break him down; however, over time, his health failed and he began to grow weak. Twelve years later, on December 9, 2017, after multiple test were run and tumors had been found, we stood in a place of shock, hearing that my father was very ill with cancer. I was devastated. "Not again!! I can't lose both my parents!! I've already lost my Mother, do I have to lose my Father too?" I began to reflect on who my Father had become since my Mother's death. Throughout the years after my wonderful, sweet mother's passing, I saw my Father change for the better. It was easy to see that he missed her dearly and I could tell my Dad knew what he had lost. His heart softened in every area and I could see a move of God in his life. When he needed prayer, he was open to receiving it. I got the courage to pray with my Dad on a few occasions, and even got him to like my smoothies and some of my vegetarian food. It was great to hear him ask for more, as I laughed and said "I knew you would like it."

I had two children by now, who loved their "Papa." He was a PROUD Grandpa and Papa! My Dad would call us from Atlanta every few days, or a couple times a week for years just to say "Hi, how ya doin? How's my grandson and granddaughter doin?" It wouldn't be a long conversation, but it meant the world to me. I would joke with him about the amount of time we would spend on the phone in conversation, he would laugh and say "Alright, hold it down." Every year for my birthday, after my mom died, my dad called in the early morning to say "Happy Birthday!" These beautiful moments ran through my mind like a flood. I tried so frantically to hold on to each memory as I stood there in that hospital trying not to succumb to the feelings of desperation and fear that gripped me.

The diagnosis was a true shock to all of us. Anger crept in immediately. Why Lord? I couldn't let my faith waiver. I truly had to push to fight in prayer. I had to fight to use this as an opportunity to support my dad in what he wanted. My Father was ready to FIGHT this. I don't think he knew what he was in for, but I was hopeful for God's hand to work mightily. At this time in my life, my walk with the Lord was stronger, more grounded, and my walk lined up more with the Word than it had ever been before. We were ready to fight! Here we go devil! I was faithfully calling every day, every other day, to check on him and talk to him. I had to settle for phone calls since I didn't live there. This was the one time that I wished I lived closer to my Father. Being in Chicago seemed millions of miles away from Atlanta. Even over the phone it wasn't hard to notice that he was growing weaker. Where my Father was once able to walk, he now needed assistance, he was losing his eyesight completely, but he still wanted to fight. He was just as FIESTY as he was before the diagnosis, even though his body was letting him down. From afar I learned of the decline, and when I went down in February again to help, I could see the decline with my own eyes. This was so hard to watch, to visibly see my Father's body break down on him.

My Father died March 3, 2018. I had been there with him by his side about two hours before he transitioned. As I was getting up to leave to catch a plane back to Chicago, I whispered to him "I love you Dad and I'll be back tomorrow," and as I was waiting at the airport to head back home he took his last breath. Though I knew he was coming to his end here on earth, I just wanted a little more time with him. There I was crying like a baby yet again. First my Mother, now my Father. I already missed him, the sound of his voice and the light banter between us. I knew he was with the Lord, so that was some solace for me, but I wanted to be there by his side when he departed, but I was at the airport. Now he's gone.

He remained strong until his last breath. Though his earthly body had let him down, he was still strong in spirit and mighty. In the last week of his life on earth, though he was weak and had not drank any water or eaten any food, he was able to grab and pull himself to turn to the side. This mere feat of turning over, something we do without thinking, took so much for him to do. The strength he had at that moment was a transformative example for me to know and realize that when I think I am at my weakest, I am strong in the Lord.

I grieved differently this time around. After losing my mom, I was a wreck, didn't care and didn't know how to move on. I had to grow to see loss as something that was a part of life. I had to come to the realization that there were people dying everyday but also that new lives were born into this world every day. Though loss is NEVER easy, I came to think about it differently and talk about it in a different way as the years went by. When my Father died, I missed him and still do, I knew immediately that I would be okay and that I wouldn't be the wreck I was after my Mother passed. I cried everyday as expected, but I was able to laugh as well. I was more spiritually mature and I had come to know the Lord in a personal way which helped me to process my Father's death differently. I was still angry, but God turned my mourning into joy by that next day because I found myself smiling. God was truly a part of my being, and he was helping me heal and get through this. I am also able to help my children grieve properly over the loss of their "Papa" and give them time and space to mourn and to help them know that he is with Jesus. This is also helping me to mourn and trust God through this process.

I carry my Mother's smile and my Father's strength as I continue to walk this journey called Life. Truly, both my Mother and Father smiled, laughed, and maintained a strength beyond imagination to the end of their earthly lives. I am blown away that I had the opportunity to witness it. In the face of physical pain and the voice of doctor's words that did not line up with what they were fighting for, they were still strong. I will never forget them, and they live on in many ways, through their children, grandchildren, and extended family. My God has continued to carry me through this and I am continually amazed at the new life I have in Him.

YOU ARE NO ACCIDENT
By: Sonia Ivy

For I know the thoughts that I think toward you, saith the LORD, thoughts of peace, and not of evil, to give you an expected end. (Jeremiah 29:11)

Who am I? Why am I here? Who is God? What happens after I die? Questions, questions, and more questions. All I seem to have are questions. Questions are neither good nor bad. Questions are guides to inquiry, help, assist, and bring meaning in life. In order to arrive at certain answers, certain questions are asked. As a young girl I had no idea why I had all of these questions. I later learned my inquisitive nature is what God is nurturing in me. I call it creative curiosity. As I am maturing, I am understanding that creative curiosity is a gift from God.

My creative curiosity was heightened in 1998. It was a pleasant July summer day. The sky was picturesque, the air crisp, and my car clean. There were manicured lawns around and it seemed as if it was going to be a good day. It was me and three others cruising in my new '97 green Saturn headed to the company picnic where there would be food, fun, and friends. Enjoying time together we were talking, laughing, and listening to music. As I am driving one of the passenger's screams, "look out!" I look to the left of me and all of a sudden, the scene went into slow motion. Another driver had run the stop sign and was headed straight for my car. It was too late to try to stop or speed up. As I turned to look it was lights out, for me!

When I woke, I remembered seeing the other passengers, paramedics, ambulance, fire department, police, and my family who had arrived at the scene of the accident. I do not know how long I was unconscious. I was more concerned about the passengers in my car than I was about myself. The paramedics where asking me my name, date of birth, and if I remembered what happened? Little did I know, at the time of the impact, I too became impacted. This included an impact where the driver hit the driver's side of my car and I hit a brick marquee. I remember my dad thinking that I was dead because of how damaged my car looked. My new car was crushed but no one else was hurt!

I was immediately rushed to the hospital where a series of tests were done. Sometime later that day, my oldest brother Terry arrived at the hospital and surprised me with a giant chocolate chip cookie. I spent one night in the hospital for observation and was released to go home the next day. I left the hospital with minor bruises and back pain along with a few stitches on my chin. I went to physical therapy for my back and with time, my back was healing and I was growing stronger. I did not know that this accident would bring with it another level of creative curiosity.

Today, it has been exactly 20 years from the date of the accident and with hindsight, I am able to see a timeline that displays maturing mile markers. I now see the love of God! What God is doing is braiding in the different fabrics of my life through time and experiences. I realize that my creative curiosity are questions about purpose. I can only know the answers to such questions as I grow to know God. For my identity and purpose are one in the same. After, the accident the questions changed. Why am I still living? What is my purpose? Why didn't I die?

The Lord keeps reminding me that I am no accident! That my identity and purpose are hidden in His Son Jesus Christ. I am a beloved daughter of the King. The reason I did not die in that accident is to bring glory to God. This accident is a part of my story. It causes me to remember my past in comparison to where I am now. I remember when I started out with just questions. Little girl questions, teenage questions, young adult questions. These questions of love and life have grown deeper in time from childhood to adulthood. Considering all of these questions, what matters the most is God's love for me.

Life does not just happen. Time is not stagnant. Change is presented to those who grab it. I am in eager expectation to see the results of a purposed life. In Jeremiah 29:11 is a promise that says, *For I know the thoughts that I think toward you, saith the Lord, thoughts of peace, and not of evil, to give you an expected end.* The purpose God has for me are expressed thoughts of creative curiosity.

Leaving It All to Follow Jesus
By: Mandy Garcia

And every one that hath forsaken houses, or brethren, or sisters, or father, or mother, or wife, or children, or lands, for my name's sake, shall receive an hundredfold, and shall inherit everlasting life. (Matthew 19:29)

Have you ever asked yourself what would happen if you had to let everything go? Would you? This is the exact situation I found myself in not long ago. Sitting in a room with my clothes in baskets and my children looking up at me with wonder in their eyes. They were just as confused as me. What's next…?

Growing up, I did not know the Lord. I didn't grow up in the church or a Christian household. By the time I was 24 years old I had three kids and lived with my boyfriend. Even though he grew up in church, we didn't go to church together. My children began to go to church with my close friend and they really seemed to enjoy it. I thought, Wow! My kids are going to church and I'm not. At this point my boyfriend and I would go to his church, but then he stopped. I started going with my kids (to their church) and learned something new, real and eye opening. The more I went, the more my eyes were opened to the truth. I then accepted Jesus as my Savior and started going to church and bible study regularly. The closer I drew to the Lord, the further apart my boyfriend and I became. I've lost a few friends as well. Not only were my eyes opened to the truth of God's Word and his love for me, but my eyes were opened to how bad my relationship was in reality. All of the arguing, fighting and bitterness no longer seemed normal, but unhealthy and toxic. I stayed for way too long, expecting things to change, seeking counseling, trying to be supportive, but nothing seemed to help. We started out together and on the same page, but we kept growing further and further apart. I was drained emotionally and did not want to be at home. The longer I stayed, the more I was convinced to leave and step out on faith.

I knew God loved me and wanted more for my life. I eventually got to the point where anything would be better than this! I went from not knowing who God was to giving him all of me! I knew that being in this relationship did not honor him at all. I finally got to the point that what I wanted most in life was to honor him, even if it meant leaving my home and going to a shelter.

When I walked through those doors with my bags and three children in tow, all I could think about was how I was at peace. Before I made the decision to go to a shelter, I prayed like never before. I wanted to make sure this is where God wanted me. Who would have known that my faith would be so strong that I felt at peace in a shelter! I now understand why my story is not to be kept a secret, but shared without shame.

While in the shelter, I spoke with women who were in way more difficult situations than mine. I would talk with them and even prayed for some. I couldn't believe I was praying for other people!!

Meanwhile, my kids and I got up every day and continued to have the most normal life possible. We went to school, work and church, leaning on God every day. My only struggle was thinking that I let my kids down because a shelter is not a good place for children. Though this is what I said at the time, I came to terms with the situation as a life lesson for us all. We were all learning to trust God in the good times and the bad and believe that his way is better even when it doesn't look or feel like it.

About a week into our stay, I started to call around for a place to live. "Hello! I'm a single mom and…" That's all I could get out before it got real. No one wanted a woman with one income and kids. I was turned down left and right for three weeks. I would get discouraged and cry wondering if I made the right decision to leave everything. It was also during that time my good friend was diagnosed with cancer and I had no one to talk to or lean on, at least that's what I told myself.

I finally got a hold of this man's number who had an apartment available. When I went to meet with him I humbled myself and poured out to him about where I was living, how I was trying to change my life, and how I wouldn't let him down. I was willing to do anything within reason to put my children in a home that was near their schools, as I didn't want to further complicate their lives more than I had already. The man heard everything I was saying and told me he would give me a chance and have a house for me to live in about three weeks. At the time, it seemed like forever, but I spent a lot of my time in the hospital with my friend. She was dying and all I could do was sit with her and pray over her as much as I could. I'm sad to say that I lost my friend during that time.

The good news is when I got my key, everything started to come together for me. There was never a time where God left me hanging, I had no worries at all and made it through the hardest time of my life. Our new home was much better than our apartment and we are so much happier! For all of you who think you can't leave or you will fail, stay strong and lean on God at all times. Don't take anything that God did not intend for you. Remember, women are powerful, purposeful and precious in God!!!!

We Are Precious In His Sight
Questions for Reflection/Discussion

1. Define the word love. What does it mean to you? Do you believe God loves you? Why? What scriptures signify his love toward you?

2. Think about all of your bad relationships. How did you make the decision to enter into said relationship? How/Why did you ultimately get out? Is your current relationship pleasing to God? Why? Why not?

3. Find a biblical example of someone making a terrible decision (there are plenty). What was the result of that decision? What did the Lord do about it? What lessons can be gleaned from their folly?

4. Reflect on your life before you knew the Lord. What was your behavior, thoughts or actions before you realized God had a better way? What made you decide to choose Him? How has your life changed?

5. Choose an author from this Section of the book whose story resonates with you. Why is their story meaningful to you? How would you handle the situation if you were in their shoes?

6. Write down areas of your life that you want to change. Why do you want this change? What scriptures do you have to aid in this change?

7. Make a decision to accept the love of God and His way for your life. Read Psalm 138 and believe that God will complete His purpose for you because you are precious to Him!

Epilogue

Let us hear the conclusion of the whole matter: Fear God, and keep his commandments: for this is the whole duty of man. (Ecclesiastes 12:13)

    The Women of this Volume experienced many trials and tribulations; from car accidents, tumors, rape, disease, drug abuse, and domestic violence, to financial lack, barrenness, fear, unbelief and rebellion. Yet the Lord delivered us all! The most amazing aspect of these testimonials is that this is not the sum total of our experiences with the power of God. If we all wrote about the innumerable times the Lord delivered us, there would not be enough volumes to contain them! The bible is clear about that!

And there are also many other things which Jesus did, the which, if they should be written every one, I suppose that even the world itself could not contain the books that should be written. Amen. (John 21:25)

    Jesus performed many miracles during bible times and He's still performing them today. He's the same yesterday, today and forever. (Hebrews 13:8) You needn't go further than the mirror to see a living, breathing, walking, talking miracle! You are a testimony! If you learn nothing else from this book, know this: The Lord has been saving you from dangers seen and unseen, making provision for you in countless ways, and showing you favor when you least deserve it, all to draw you closer and show you that you can and should trust Him.

The real conclusion of the matter is that life happens. People live and die, doors open and shut and things often do not turn out as planned. Typically, at the exact moment you feel like everything is going well, things fall apart. What do you do when things fall apart? You fear God and keep his commandments. Well, Tiffany, how exactly do I accomplish that in the face of dire circumstances you ask? First, you fear God. To Fear God means to revere, reverence and be in awe of Him. We surrender to Him as the greater power and authority. We give no credence to fear because fear seeks to immobilize and debilitate you by exalting your weaknesses above your strengths. When you reverence God and His Word over fear you will hear the Word say, *My grace is sufficient for thee: for my strength is made perfect in weakness* (2 Cor. 12:9). God's grace is more than enough for you to overcome any obstacle or adverse circumstance in your life. Receive His grace, just as the women in this Volume did, even when they didn't realize it, they were recipients of the grace and mercy of a loving God whose strength was made perfect in their weaknesses.

The second thing you do is keep his commandments. The way you keep his commandments is by learning to trust the Lord in EVERY thing. The bible says, *Trust in the Lord with all thine heart; and lean not unto thine own understanding. In all thy ways acknowledge him, and he shall direct thy paths.* (Proverbs 3: 5, 6) We must learn to acknowledge the Lord in ALL of our ways, not just some. The word acknowledge in this passage (Hebrew word *yada*) means not to just speak His name as a form of giving lip service to him, but a genuine knowing of who he is and his desired outcome of a situation. Jesus framed it best when he taught the disciples

Epilogue

to pray in Matthew 6:10. He said, "Thy kingdom come. Thy will be done in earth, as it is in heaven." We want our situation on earth to look like the King and his Kingdom has intervened on our behalf. This is how we truly acknowledge the Lord in all of our ways. Every time you have more month than money, say, "Your kingdom come, your will be done in my life, as it is in heaven." Every time sickness or disease rears its ugly head, say, "Your kingdom come, your will be done in my body, as it is in heaven." Every time your children behave like they were raised by Neanderthals and not you, say, "Your kingdom come, your will be done in my children, as it is in heaven." You get the idea. We must learn to trust God and stand on His word at all times, every time.

When you have a lifestyle of acknowledging the Father, you will have a history of Him directing your path. When He directs your path, you will know He is with you, even if you walk through the valley of the shadow of death you will fear no evil (Psalm 23:4), just Him. When you fear him, you will keep his commandments and live an abundant life through Him.

Take some time to ponder the path of your feet (Proverbs 4:26) and you will see how far you have come in life. When you ponder over your life, you will see how God's grace preserved you, His mercy saved you and His love covered your sins (Proverbs 10:12). When you have indeed been covered by the love of the Father, you realize that you too *Do Not Look Like What You've Been Through* and you have a powerful testimony through Christ Jesus our Lord!

www.ingramcontent.com/pod-product-compliance
Lightning Source LLC
LaVergne TN
LVHW051604070426
835507LV00021B/2758

www.ingramcontent.com/pod-product-compliance
Lightning Source LLC
LaVergne TN
LVHW051606070426
835507LV00021B/2791